Praise for *Ease*

"Rooted in science, research, and common sense, *Ease* is a powerful and thoughtful book to help us all manage our frenetic lives. Best of all, it reads like you're in the room, one-on-one, with coaching pro Eileen Chadnick. And I can tell you from personal experience, that's a wonderful place to be."

- **Terry Fallis**, award-winning author of *The Best Laid Plans*, and co-founder of Thornley Fallis Communications

"Eileen has done us busy people an enormous service with *Ease*. It is quite one thing to know what the neuroscience and positive psychology research says about dealing with times of "crazy busy" but quite another to apply the strategies to our own lives. Eileen bridges both and lays out a smorgasbord of solid ideas that are easy to grasp and to customize to one's own needs. This deceptively simple yet profoundly informed book will make a difference for me and for others who read it. The positive frame and good writing make me feel better already just from reading it."

- **Linda J. Page**, PhD, President of Adler International and co-author of *Coaching With the Brain in Mind*

"Struggle is strictly overrated! Sure, you're busy, but are you being EFFECTIVE? *Ease* is a practical, grounded book and a treasure chest of do-able exercises that will help you focus, maximize and do what you can do."

- **Kim George**, author, *Coaching Into Greatness: 4 Steps to Success in Business and Life*, Founder, The Abundance Intelligence Institute® www.AbundanceIntelligence.com

"The science tells us that if we can manage our stress, our sleep and our mood we can boost our capacity to have more impact; work with a greater sense of ease; and do more Great Work. Easy to say, much harder to do. Eileen Chadnick lays out 17 practical tools so you can move from insight to action ... and start to experience a real difference."

- **Michael Bungay Stanier**, Senior Partner of Box of Crayons and author of *Do More Great Work*

E A S E

MANAGE OVERWHELM IN TIMES OF "CRAZY BUSY"

EILEEN CHADNICK

iUniverse LLC
Bloomington

EASE
MANAGE OVERWHELM IN TIMES OF "CRAZY BUSY"

iUniverse books may be ordered through booksellers or by contacting:

iUniverse
1663 Liberty Drive
Bloomington, IN 47403
www.iuniverse.com
1-800-Authors (1-800-288-4677)

Because of the dynamic nature of the Internet, any web addresses or links contained in this book may have changed since publication and may no longer be valid. The views expressed in this work are solely those of the author and do not necessarily reflect the views of the publisher, and the publisher hereby disclaims any responsibility for them.

Any people depicted in stock imagery provided by Thinkstock are models, and such images are being used for illustrative purposes only.
Certain stock imagery © Thinkstock.

ISBN: 978-1-4917-0935-1 (sc)
ISBN: 978-1-4917-0937-5 (hc)
ISBN: 978-1-4917-0936-8 (e)

Library of Congress Control Number: 2013917159

Printed in the United States of America.

iUniverse rev. date: 10/31/2013

To Sam and Sylvia Chadnick, I am eternally grateful for who you are and for how you have helped me become who I am today.

Ease.

To free from something that pains, disquiets, or burdens
To take away or lessen, alleviate
To give freedom or relief (as from pain or discomfort)[1]

Well-being.

The state of being happy, healthy, or prosperous[2]

Contents

Part III: What's Next?

Part I: Managing with Ease in Times of "Crazy Busy"

Chapter 1
Introduction

The Blur

Get to office for early morning meeting. Check the fifty-four emails that came in since last night. Book flight for business trip next week. Finish proposal. Complete performance-review notes. Talk to colleague about key deliverables due today. Attend strategic-planning session. Prepare analysis. Pick up dry-cleaning. Get kids to soccer game. Buy flowers and card for anniversary. Start research on residences for Mom. Call Realtor. Prep for tomorrow's work. Review notes for volunteer board meeting. Buy dog food, and call vet. Bring car in for tune-up. Schedule vet appointment ... !@!#

Ever Feel like Life Is a Blur?

Do you ever find yourself asking, "Where did the day go? Where did the week go? Where did the years go?" Do you look at the stuff you have to do and ask, "How the heck will I get all this done? How will I survive this week, month, year? Where did all the fun go?"

Do you sometimes feel bogged down and overwhelmed by it all?

I do. We live in times of unprecedented busyness. The demands and pace of work and life are at an all-time high, and they don't appear to be slowing down anytime soon. Work is frenetic. Change is constant. And life is as well. We are juggling it all: careers, families, volunteer and personal pursuits, and more!

Of course, the busy factor is not all imposed on us. We choose much of what's on our plate. If you are like me, you *want* to work hard, produce, and contribute. You want your life to include family, friends, meaningful pursuits, hobbies, volunteering, and learning. You want it all. Why, oh, why can't we have a nine-day week to fit it all in?

Whether our loads are self-imposed or put on us, many of us are doing our best to squeeze it all in, and we're starting to burst at the seams.

I wrote this book because I found myself feeling overwhelmed more often than I'd like, and I noticed that far too many others felt this way as well. While many of my clients come to me for different agendas related to their careers, lives, or leadership development, all too often, the theme of feeling overwhelmed comes up. Many people struggle with the following thoughts: *How will I get this done? The pace is just getting unbearable. I have no time. I'm exhausted*—and more.

I'm not referring to laggards or people who can't cope—quite the opposite, in fact. They (and I) are successful and accomplished professionals who are getting things done, stretching and adapting to ever-increasing change—but at a cost. In times of sustained "crazy busy," the feeling of overload has become an equal-opportunity issue for leaders and others alike. It's taking a toll on far too many of us.

In March 2012, I had an opportunity to suggest a theme for a webinar I was to present to members of the accountancy profession in Canada. Hosted by the Canadian Institute of Chartered Accountants (CICA), now called Chartered Professional Accountants of Canada (CPA), the opportunity was to focus on either a personal or professional development issue. I suggested the topic "Bogged Down with Too Much to Do? Tips and Strategies for Handling It." The timing was just before the cusp of tax season, so I didn't know if tax professionals would take an hour out of their day to listen to what they might consider a soft topic. However, more than 3,500 people registered for the presentation! Afterwards, I received scores of emails acknowledging the value of the tips and asking me for more.

This response affirmed to me that the issue of overwhelm was becoming even more salient than I had imagined.

Are Times of "Crazy Busy" Now the New Normal?

We used to have seasons that were busier than others. Today, it seems every day is the season of rush. We might not notice this, because we hunker down and focus on the demands of the day. Perhaps you are doing much of what you set out to do. But underneath the surface of high performance, perhaps you are noticing a few signs of wear and tear on your personal and professional well-being. The damage might be subtle—like a small crack in veneer.

Do you recognize this in your own life? Ask yourself these questions:

Do you catch yourself feeling more bogged down than inspired or energized? Do you find yourself saying you will catch your breath once this one last project is complete, but then, no sooner than the project (or particular life challenge) ends, you are on to the next one and once again hope for that day when you'll catch your breath? Have you accidentally missed any appointments lately? Or woken up and suddenly realized you had a meeting scheduled that day, but because you forgot, you were not prepared? How's your reservoir of creativity, resourcefulness, and energy? Feeling a bit depleted? What about sleep? Are you having trouble getting enough sleep? Staying asleep? Getting quality sleep? And how's that affecting your work? Your mood? Your sense of well-being?

Perhaps it's time for something different.

When I owned up to the fact that I had been working and living with what I refer to as "overwhelm static" in my life for too long, I knew I needed to change something. I didn't want to disengage from the activities of my life; I have goals, plans, and dreams, and I want to work hard and live full out. But I also knew I wanted to feel more at peace and energized on a more sustained and consistent basis. I wanted to work hard but with fewer struggles.

I wanted to feel more ease in my life. And I have had many clients who have expressed this same desire.

Interestingly, the definition of *ease* is to remove what burdens us.

Ease.

To free from something that pains, disquiets, or burdens
To take away or lessen, alleviate
To give freedom or relief (as from pain or discomfort) [1]

Life isn't going to slow down; the pressures will likely continue. So we have to adapt. Realistically, it wouldn't be possible to simply remove all sources of burden, but we can learn new ways to engage with them and with ourselves to create more ease.

But I want more than that—more than simply removing burden. Our brains, bodies, and spirits need to work *towards* something, not just *away* from something. I want to up the ante on well-being.

Well-being.

The state of being happy, healthy, or prosperous [2]

How to work and live with more ease and experience greater well-being— that's what this book is all about.

The heart of this book is a toolkit filled with strategies and ideas to navigate the demands of work and life with more ease and well-being.

Like you, I live a fluid, dynamic life and recognize there is always room for improvement. In looking closely at my own habits, I found many strengths that were helping me, but I also discovered gaps that were like leaks in my own well-being bucket. I bet this is the same for many of you. I see this with my clients. We do a lot right, but some of our habits (or non-habits) can become a critical source of drain on energy, resilience, and potential to be fulfilled. From my experiences in my life and with clients, I compiled a volume of strategies and ideas that I refer to as tools.

None of the ideas I offer are difficult or complex. In fact, some are embarrassingly simple and might be reminders of what you already know. Yet despite their simplicity, they work.

The rationale behind most of the ideas (i.e., tools) I present draws from an army of expertise from the fields of positive psychology, neuroscience, leadership, emotional intelligence, coaching, and more. Some are my own, and some come from others. All have been tried and tested in the field and also in my own "kitchen"—with myself and hundreds of clients over the years.

I would have liked to write a book that promised three easy steps to wipe out overwhelm—it would have sold millions! But I know better. This business of overwhelm is multifaceted and personal to each individual. This book does not offer a prescribed system. Each individual is unique and most likely will need to tap into different areas for his or her own situation. So rather than a prescription, I provided a toolkit—a repository of ideas and tips that can be customized into your own personal well-being plan.

Here's what you'll find in this book:

Deconstructing Overwhelm: The first thing we are going to do is get our arms around understanding overwhelm from a mind-brain perspective. Many of the strategies (i.e., tools) are designed around current understanding related to the mind-brain connection. I'm sure you've heard the expression "It's all in your mind." Well, this is quite right. But that doesn't mean it's in your imagination and not real to you. Our brains and minds are powerful forces, and we need to better understand them so that we can intentionally work with them rather than against them if we are to experience more ease, success, and fulfilment. Despite the simplicity of the tools presented, there is a backbone of some neuroscience, some mindfulness, and both emotional and positive intelligence supporting the ideas.

Toolkit: The toolkit is designed around a few major themes, and together, these themes round out a holistic approach to working and living with more ease and experiencing well-being during times of "crazy busy." The three main themes include the following:

Mind Full? Organize and Focus with the Brain in Mind
Mindful: Develop Conscious and Empowering Mindsets
Mood Matters: Hone the Positivity Advantage

Being mindful is essential to working with more ease and experiencing greater success and well-being. The opposite—having an overly distracted or excessively full mind—can lead to a first-class ticket to feeling frazzled and overwhelmed. Our starting focus in the toolkit will be to help you manage the volume of stuff on your plate (and in your head!) so as to avoid that trap.

Next we'll move on to developing more empowering thinking strategies. Being mindful is no longer the exclusive domain of Buddhists. Anyone who wants to be on his or her best game needs to make the mind a friend, not a foe. In this section, we will dive into strategies to develop conscious mindsets that can create powerful shifts in how we engage with ourselves and the challenges present in work and life. Small shifts in perspective can powerfully boost our capacity to get things done—and with more resilience, optimism, and creativity. This mindset is not only about being more effective; these mindful approaches are also brain-friendly ways to manage the biological responses that occur with stress and reap the rewards of more conscious, reflective mindsets.

In the last part of the toolkit, we will focus on developing positivity habits. Once upon a time, it was a guilty pleasure to pursue happiness and fulfilment. Now there is a bounty of research affirming how important positivity is for our mental, emotional, and physical well-being and our ability to flourish at work and in life, especially in times of challenge. We'll explore some of the essential habits that come from fields of emotional intelligence and positive psychology. These tools are easy to do and offer powerful results.

Along the way, you will meet some people in the "Stories at a Glance" sections. In some of the stories, the individuals and issues represent aggregates of clients or people I know; in other cases, the stories come from a particular individual. In most cases, I have changed their names to protect their identities. I've also shared many of my own personal stories too—even a few embarrassing ones!

The parts of this book are intentionally not assembled. The game plan is to give you ideas that you can choose from to meet your personal needs. In the last section of this book, I will offer you additional exercises and further guidance to help you create a customized approach that works for you. You can draw on the ideas that resonate with you to design your own personal well-being plan.

This book is for you if ...

✓ You find yourself feeling bogged down more often than you would like.

✓ You wanted it all but now find it increasingly more difficult to do it all.

✓ You are successful and can handle a lot, but you could use an energizing spark.

✓ You see challenges and opportunities ahead and want to take them on with gusto, but you are wondering if you can handle any more beyond what is already on your plate.

✓ You don't want to step down your game; you would rather step it up, but you will need a heartier, more productive, and more resilient you to achieve that goal.

✓ You manage to get through your days okay but lately have been having trouble sleeping, which is threatening your capacity.

If you identify with any or all of the points above, then welcome aboard. And get in line—right beside me. Remember, I'm with you on this journey of taming overwhelm and living with more ease and well-being.

Chapter 2
Deconstructing Overwhelm

Overwhelm erodes our well-being—our ability to flourish personally, professionally, and organizationally. Running too long on overload can derail even the most successful among us. It is also important to recognize that overwhelm angst is an equal-opportunity player and, increasingly, a reality for all, including leaders and high performers. People who set their sights high and engage fully in work and life are prime candidates, as they take on increasing loads with equally high expectations for handling it all.

Is this mind over matter, or is something else going on? Naysayers (or perhaps even your own internal voice of judgment) might say, "This is all in your head. Get over it!" Well, in reference to this feeling being in your head, you might be right—at least partially. There certainly is a mind-brain-overwhelm connection. But can we say it's not real if it's in our head? I don't think so. The feelings of overwhelm are not imagined, nor are the consequences. In fact, something very real is going on.

It is helpful to understand the experience of overwhelm from a brain and mind perspective. The last decade has seen a groundswell of research revealing a much greater understanding of how our brains operate and influence our abilities for thinking, feeling, responding to and managing stress, and so much more. Advancements in fields such as neuroscience, emotional intelligence, leadership, and positive psychology have opened up the doors to a significantly greater grasp of what the necessary conditions are for flourishing and, on the flip side, the derailers that impede us. It's a complex world out there, and survival of the fittest now means we need robust emotional, mental, and physical fitness to successfully navigate the challenges of work and life.

The mind-brain connection is central to all of this. Let's look at a couple key concepts related to our brains so that we can set the foundation for the ideas and strategies introduced in the toolbox.

Your Brain: The Original Model

When we consider the evolution of our brains, there's good news and bad news. First, the good news: in the last decade or so, research has revealed that our brains have a lot more plasticity than we once thought possible. This means that our brains can adapt and create new neuropaths (connections) that can be helpful in developing new habits and ways of thinking and feeling. This is fantastic news for anyone wanting to learn new ways to cope with challenging work and life demands and to feel more positive about his or her life. It's because of this plasticity and the ability to change the brain (with new habits) that many of the tools you'll read about in the toolbox have proven their worth. The unfortunate news is that despite the brain's ability to adapt, we are still working with the original-model brain that our ancestors had, which served well in the days of hunting-and-gathering society.

This means you are working with a brain operating system 1.0. Unlike your last computer purchase, our brain's essential operating systems have not changed since the beginning of time. In the days when we had to hunt for food, we had to contend with constant life-threatening risks, such as lions, tigers, and bears (oh my!). Our brains were—and still are—wired to scan for and protect us against those threats. The amygdala, part of the brain in the limbic system, is primed to detect any hint of danger and protect us by instantaneously preparing us for fight or flight. This is our fast brain, and the reaction it incurs is known as the stress response. Our amygdala reacts immediately and catalyzes critical biological reactions, such as the release of cortisol and adrenaline, to enable us to run, fight, and survive. The operative word here is *react*.

In contrast, in our modern-day and knowledge-based economy, most people spend their work days thinking and relating with people, ideas, and information. These tasks are different from hunting. While we still need the good work of the amygdala to protect us in the face of danger, most perceived threats of the day (toxic bosses, unreasonable workloads, busy lives at home) don't compare with sabre-toothed cats. But our brains don't know or care about that —that is, unless we get our higher-thinking brain wired up.

Meet your higher-thinking brain. In simplistic terms, the prefrontal cortex drives much of our higher-thinking brain functions. This is the part of the brain that helps us with tasks such as problem solving, analyzing, prioritizing, distinguishing, and reflecting. Unfortunately, this part of our brain works best when there are no threats—or, rather, no *perceived* threats. When we perceive risk, we send an alert signal to the fast brain (amygdala), which quickly shifts gears and gets priority over anything else. When the amygdala is fired up, it tends to suppress the prefrontal cortex (higher-thinking brain). An interesting metaphor is to picture yourself trying to think about something that requires concentration while a fire alarm is blasting.

Survival always trumps thoughtful reflection.

Is That a Tiger or a Deadline and Demanding Boss?
The amygdala (fast, or survival, brain) doesn't distinguish between perceived threats and real ones that truly threaten our survival (e.g., lions, tigers, and bears). When we feel overwhelmed by a situation and feel frightened, our emotional mind tells our brain there is a threat, and the brain shifts into high gear. Our thinking brain takes a back seat to our survival brain.

Bye-Bye, Thinking Capacity—Hello, Brain Freeze!
Do smart people suddenly become dumb when stressed out? Not really. But in the moment, it might appear so because the survival part of our

brain (amygdala) takes precedence, and it becomes more difficult to access the critical and reflective type of thinking skills we need to handle the situation that prompted the stress trigger.

The Story at a Glance

To put this information into context, let's look at a story about Brad.

> Brad is a VP managing a consulting department that recently grew from eight direct reports to fifteen and is soon to expand to twenty-five people. The company is on an ambitious growth agenda. Brad has been known to do great work, and while he confesses to not being the most organized person, he has always prided himself on having a great memory and ability to keep things together. His staff likes him. But lately, with the change of pace and increased workload, he is showing signs of wearing down. He seems to be hanging on okay, but he has a feeling that he has little battery life left in his mind, body, and spirit. Brad is worrying more and is anxious about the prospect of another increase in workload. He is not sleeping well. Usually a jovial guy, he's been feeling cranky lately, and his energy and focus are a bit off. Recently, he was asked to provide input in a situation that needed a fairly timely response and a high-level recommendation. Normally, the scenario would have been a piece of cake for Brad, as he's been known to be a sharp and quick thinker, a good strategist, and a strong problem solver. This time, his response was quite different.
>
> Brad froze. His brain seemed to go on vacation. He couldn't quite get his mind wrapped around the issue, and he came up empty. In a busy week, with so many balls in the air, Brad saw this request as a final straw, and he felt he just couldn't work his way through one more thinking task.

Sound familiar?

What really happened? Brad was likely experiencing an episode of overwhelm. His emotional reaction (overwhelm) to the last demand sent the prefrontal cortex (the higher-thinking brain) on holiday and kicked in another essential part of his brain to do what it was told to do: survive.

This process happened unconsciously, of course. Brad's reaction ("Oh bleep, not another task!") sent a message to his brain that he was under serious threat. So his brain did exactly what it was supposed to do when under threat: it suppressed the reflective, problem-solving side of the brain, which Brad would have needed to respond to the business request, and kick-started the other part of his brain that was built to protect.

It was the wrong response for the situation but the right reaction, given Brad's signal.

Brad's brain went into fight-or-flight mode—at the expense of his thinking capacity. His levels of adrenaline and cortisol kicked in aggressively and started revving the stress engine. Perhaps if he had been able to mentally process the last request, he might not have felt as threatened by the request. Or if he'd taken time to pause in order to self-manage his reaction, he might have been able to moderate his sense of threat, which would have enabled him to access his resourceful, creative, sharp-thinking self. There are many strategies we could recommend to Brad to help tame that stress response, but for now, the key is to understand what happened from a mind-brain perspective.

While our *brains* might not know the difference between a deadline and a tiger, we can influence and manage our *minds* by choosing thoughts that will be more productive to the situation. Another way of putting this: we can self-manage our emotional and thinking responses so as not to automatically trigger the biological stress response. And at the same time, we can learn practical strategies to better organize and handle our loads so that we reduce the chance of triggering our mind's negative, threat-based reactions.

> **The Mind-Brain Connection**
> *While our brains might be built to react in a particular way, we can learn to better manage our mind's reactions, which influence the message sent to the brain. Developing habits to tame the mind is the crux of more emotionally intelligent behaviour and the foundation for many of the tools in this book.*

There's more that might help explain Brad's experience of brain freeze. Let's look at a concept from the world of neuroleadership[1] that is useful to help understand what might be going on for Brad—and for yourself!

The term "leadership lockdown syndrome"[2] was coined by neuroscientists Jessica Payne and Stephen Thomas for a presentation made at the NeuroLeadership conference in 2011.[3] According to the summary outlined in the NeuroLeadership Institute's blog article, Payne and Thomas were researching the neural needs and resources of successful senior leaders and identified three things the brain needs to function optimally: moderate stress, good sleep, and positive affect (positive mood). In today's high-pressure work world, meeting these three needs is not as simple as it sounds. When a leader simultaneously experiences high stress, poor sleep, and negative mood, it can be a perfect storm that greatly compromises one's critical thinking capacity.

The three areas cited do not stand in isolation. They are interconnected. High stress hinders sleep and positive affect (mood). Poor sleep makes it difficult to manage stress and maintain a positive mood. And negative mood tends to make sleep and stress worse. So when people experience all three together, the interaction can result in overly stressful reactions, cognitive impairment, and a compromise in basic perception, judgment, and decision-making abilities.

Insufficient sleep also means we are not giving our brains time to integrate information in a meaningful way and are therefore operating at a suboptimal level, especially with regard to creativity. Sleep also plays a big role in regulating emotions, a crucial strength for any executive.

This makes a lot of sense. I know that when I am tired due to poor sleep, I can't trust my judgment nor my mood. And when I'm stressed, the stress often gets in the way of my sleep. It's a vicious circle!

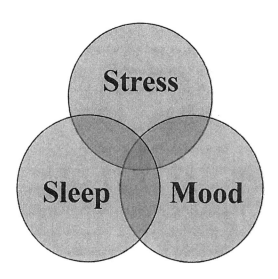

If you recall, Brad was trying to stay on top of things and relying on his memory. But after a certain point, this wasn't working for him. He was worrying more (experiencing more stress), not sleeping, and getting cranky. Was he experiencing leadership lockdown syndrome? Possibly. A task that normally would have been completely manageable for Brad was too difficult.

So who is vulnerable to experiencing something like this? I don't think you have to be in a formal leadership role to experience this. I would imagine anyone who is challenged in these three areas would experience similar reactions. The essential point is to learn to moderate our stress levels; to ensure we get ample sleep (which is not so easy for many— we'll get to that later); and to learn to develop more positivity, which contributes greatly to our higher-thinking capacity and our ability to maintain resilience even when dealing with stress and challenging demands in work and life.

Emotional and Positive Intelligence at Work

To be able to successfully navigate the complex and accelerating demands of work and life, we need skills—not just the technical skills of your work but also mental, personal, and emotional skills. These skills come from the realms of both emotional intelligence and positive intelligence. Abilities related to practising self-awareness and self-management, handling stress, dealing with people, and coping with the uncertainty and complexity of work and life are now increasingly valued as key leadership and workforce competencies.

Likewise, the importance of mood (positivity) can't be understated. Research continues to affirm that positively oriented people are more apt to be successful in their work and lives and in coping with the challenges and adversity that come their way. Positivity not only makes us feel better but also has been proven to improve our thinking abilities, which we need in order to handle complex work and life demands.

The good news is that you can develop skills related to emotional and positive intelligence. With the right practices, you can rewire your brain with more-productive thinking habits, creating new neural connections that will help you become more resilient, optimistic, and joyful.

We can't control all of our circumstances, but we can control how we engage and react to them from an emotional, mental, and mindset perspective. Your toolkit (coming up next) has been designed with all this in mind. It is laden with ideas, thoughts, and tips to help you develop a more positive and emotionally intelligent approach to your work and life.

Here are some questions that underscore the ideas you'll find in the toolkit.

- As the loads of work (and life) become heavier, and with tougher deadlines, how can we organize our stuff and ourselves in a way that is brain-friendly and allows us to handle our loads more productively and with less stress?
- If the brain can't distinguish between a lion and a tough workload, then how can we use our mind to appropriately bring that perceived threat back into its respectful cage and put the brakes on the stress response?
- If mood is central to coping, how do we get better control over our emotions to reap the rewards of the positivity advantage?
- If quality sleep is essential to our well-being and ability to cope and thrive, how do we get an ample dose of quality sleep if we are challenged in that area?

These are just a few of the questions we will address in the next sections. Let's go!

Part II: Toolkit

Chapter 3
Welcome to Your Toolkit: Operating Manual

Welcome to your toolkit! This is where you will find ideas, tips, and strategies to help tame overwhelm and bring more ease into your work and life.

As I mentioned earlier, the toolkit is not meant to be a step-by-step prescribed process. Rather, this is a repository of ideas, strategies, and tips, and you can choose the ones that most resonate with you. No one strategy will cover the whole job. Approach this as a resource that you can dip into at your own pace, and find your own mix of what might work for you now. Experiment and be open to some trial and error. Pick one or two ideas at a time, and work with them to see what happens. Then go back and try another. Small changes can add up over time to a profound impact.

Set the intention to create a customized well-being plan. Remember, your plan can evolve as you do. Towards the end of this book, you'll find additional exercises to supplement the tools in each chapter to help you craft your plan and evolve it as you go.

As you read through some of the tools, you might find that they appear simplistic and wonder if they really work. Sometimes the simple ideas are the most powerful. None of the approaches outlined are meant to be complex. In fact, many of the ideas might not even be new to you. That's okay—sometimes we need a reminder.

Keep an open mind as you read the tools. With an open mind, you might find nuggets that extend well beyond the words offered in these pages. Make them your own!

As you read the tools, keep the following questions at the front of your mind:

1. What's useful about this idea? What part, notion, or element can I use?
2. What can I do with this idea? If I can't use it exactly as offered, what would my version of this look like?
3. How can I test this? What specifically would that look like in action in my own life?
4. What am I already doing in this area, and how can I improve upon it?
5. What other ideas of my own does this tool inspire?

Chapter 4
Mind Full? Organize and Focus with the Brain in Mind

When work and life go into overdrive, it is easy to fall into the frazzle trap. As we juggle large loads, our attention gets stretched and pulled in many directions. How we react and navigate this volume of demands and complexity will determine the extent to which we feel in control or overwhelmed. When we feel a lack of control and a sense of overwhelm, we lose function in the part of the brain known as the prefrontal cortex. If you are already extremely organized, you might have a leg up on this, but for many of us, we can do better.

This section offers practical ideas (tools) to better organize ourselves in a way that works *with* our brains so that we can pre-empt the mind-full, bogged-down state of mind and shift to a more mindful (conscious and intentional) way of navigating work and life. The intent is to help you feel more in control of your time and put you back into the driver's seat of your work and life, even when demands are coming in from many directions.

Tools → Mind Full? Organize with the Brain in Mind

1. Get It out of Your Head: Write It Down
2. Get a Grip on Your Schedule
3. Prioritize and Triage
4. Manage Distractions
5. Reign In the Multitasking
6. Learn to Say No
7. Manage the Paradox of Choice at the Buffet of Life

Tool #1: Get It out of Your Head: Write It Down

"Too much to do and not enough time" is increasingly becoming the battle cry of work warriors in today's "crazy busy" environment. Many of us have an exceptional capacity to handle large loads, but there can come a tipping point where we feel as if we've got too much to handle.

The Story at a Glance

When I coach people who appear frazzled and bogged down, I often ask the following question: "What's your system for organizing yourself?" I'm not referring to any particular technology model or particular application. What I want to get at is how they keep track of the stuff they have to do (tasks, responsibilities, meetings, etc.). I'm curious if they lean towards keeping stuff in their heads (memory) or if they have structures to tangibly capture all their tasks. I might ask the following:

What kind of list(s) do you maintain to keep track of your to-dos?
How do you stay attuned to your immediate, upcoming, and longer-term priorities?
How often do you update and check your lists?
Can you see your lists at any time with ease, or are they somewhere filed away in your computer?
What do you do when ad hoc stuff comes in that isn't on the list—how does that get captured?
What do you do when stuff doesn't get done from your immediate list?

I am not a professional organizer by any means. But when working with busy people, I find it absolutely essential to explore their organizational habits when they are feeling bogged down by too much to do. While these kinds of questions might seem basic, I can't tell you how often this kind of conversation reveals a gap in a client's organizational habits. Usually, the more frazzled the person, the more gaps he or she has. What once worked to manage responsibilities might not be sufficient as the loads and pace ramp up.

Our brains love it when we make plans and get organized. It frees up our minds from heavy burdens and the discomfort of having too much to do; provides a sense of order amid the chaos that can come with today's fast-paced, high-volume work lives; and keeps us focused.

There is actually some science associated with to-do lists and other organizational strategies. When we organize, focus, and prioritize, we access our higher-thinking brain (the prefrontal cortex) and enjoy a release of a chemical called GABA (gamma-aminobutyric acid), which can provide a calming effect on the brain. In the midst of a moment of stress due to increased workload, taking a moment to refresh your to-do lists can actually be a calming experience.

Additionally, there is an interesting concept known as the Zeigarnik effect,[1] named after the Russian psychologist Bluma Zeigarnik.[2] In 1927, she discovered that people tend to remember incomplete or interrupted tasks better than completed tasks.

This means we have a tendency to dwell on (in our minds) our unfinished business. As our loads increase, without a visual form of our priorities, we tend to hold on and try to jam our task-oriented information into our short-term memory. Note the distinction between being *mind full* versus *mindful*. Trying to constantly remember what else you have to do—or worrying about it—can be energy consuming, distracting, and not a productive strategy. Have you ever been to a meeting and missed part of what was being said because you were worrying about the stuff already on your plate?

Our brains weigh about 2 per cent of the average person's body weight, yet they use about 20 per cent of our energy and nutrients to function. Our higher-thinking brain (the prefrontal cortex) has limited attention capacity to simultaneously process multiple thinking tasks. Trying to remember your to-dos is fine when you have moderate workloads, but when the ante is raised, you are wasting brainpower that can be used for other more-important thinking tasks. Remember Brad from chapter 1? He was fine with his remembering strategy until his workload and pressure increased, and then it all fell apart.

A cluttered, busy mind can also disrupt sleep. Having a system that captures your to-dos can help you focus on your tasks in the moment and alleviate monkey-mind-at-night syndrome.

So how do you balance keeping your to-dos at the top of your mind but out of your head?

The Advice

In short, the advice is to write your tasks down (in some form). Create and fine-tune structures that help you keep track of your stuff so that you can concentrate on what matters in the moment. Those who do not have appropriate organizational habits for their work and life loads find themselves more prone to experiencing chaos. Their increasing workloads trigger emotional threat responses, which further compromises the ability to think, perform, and function optimally.

While each individual might have his or her own specific approach, it is important to have something that provides a visual manifestation of all your to-dos. One simple to-do list likely won't cut it. Regardless of what structure you choose, consider these qualities:

- It is visual and not in your head. You can see it.
- You can access it quickly and easily.
- It is dynamic and flexible enough to accommodate the fluid nature of your to-dos.
- It's part of a routine, not ad hoc.
- It's simple and doesn't add more work to your load.
- It covers immediate, near-term (tomorrow and upcoming), and long-term priorities.
- It covers different dimensions of your life (personal, work, and others).

Make It Work for You

There isn't one way or a perfect way to record your responsibilities and to-dos. I've had clients who have customized this organizational tool to their style. One used a notebook (she loved paper) to draw up margins that reflected different parts of her work and life and for different time horizons (today, tomorrow, long-term). Another client used a whiteboard for the long-term to-dos. Others are finding technology applications that suit their preferences. This practice is not simply about having a system; it's about having the right system for your needs at any given time.

I confess: I am a "listaholic." My system gives me peace of mind that I will remember what I have to do, and it keeps me on track in both the short term (daily) and the long term without compromising my ability to be attentive in the moment. I am rarely surprised to see a deadline arrive out of nowhere. My lists are strategic and deliberate.

Here is a list of reminders to help you create a system that works for you.

Thirteen Ideas to Make This Work for You

1. **Reflect and rate your current organizational methods.**
    Rate their effectiveness on a scale of 1 to 10 (10 being the highest). Identify areas you can improve that are most important to you.

2. **Make sure your list (or other structure) captures stuff that you need to keep an eye on immediately (today), tomorrow, and long-term.**
    A simple daily list won't cut it.

3. **Ensure a sense of priority is reflected.**
    Consider a ranking system versus making an ad hoc, linear list. (I will say more about priorities in my discussion of the next tool.)

4. **Create a routine or ritual.**
    Doing this ad hoc isn't going to work. Identify when you will do your daily, weekly, and long-term lists. For instance, I do my daily lists at

the end of the day. It helps me complete the day and start fresh the next morning, knowing I have my priorities set.

5. **Refresh your lists as often as necessary.**
   For example, don't limit yourself to a weekly refresh just because you label a list your weekly list. On busy days that feel chaotic, I find it extremely helpful to take a few minutes to refresh my weekly list (even in the middle of the week) so that I can refocus and see what I have to deal with.

6. **Do a reality check.**
   Your list is meant to help you, not deflate you at the end of the day. Pay attention to your expectations, and check in to see if you are being realistic with what you can accomplish in a given time frame.

7. **Capture highlights only.**
   Your lists are not meant to be project-management documents.

8. **Ensure your system is easy, simple, and quick to do**.
   None of this needs to be complex. You don't want to add more work to your load. A daily list can take five minutes, and if you are regularly refreshing your weekly and long-term lists, then the refresh can be quick too.

9. **Keep your list(s) close, accessible, and easy to view and edit.**
   Overwhelm anxiety can hit at any time. Having quick access and the ability to easily view or update can be calming and allow you to feel more in control.

10. **Print out a copy of your list if it's on your computer**.
    I keep my typed-up weekly list right on my desk so that I can scribble updates on it as I go.

11. **Organize the weekly list by topic, theme, or category.**
    Try not to do a hodgepodge or a running brain dump. The brain can handle larger loads if they are in categories.

12. **Don't forget the apples!**

    This is an expression I use for ad hoc essentials that might not be work-oriented but are important. Remember, we are whole people. If picking up apples—or your spouse's anniversary gift— after work is important, then note it. Don't keep it in your head!

13. **Do a ta-da list to celebrate what you accomplished each day.**

    One of the downfalls of to-do lists is that they never end, and we tend to focus on what we haven't yet done (the Zeigarnik effect), which, in itself, can be deflating. A ta-da list is a nice antidote to this and gives a wonderful boost of accomplishment. We will revisit this idea in our section on positivity.

The Pay-Off

Instead of "Bye-bye, thinking capacity," you can say, "Hello, ease with more productivity, presence, and peace of mind!"

✓ You will feel more in control by being more organized, relieving your sense of overwhelm, and keeping your higher-thinking brain safe from an amygdala attack.

✓ It will be easier to deal with what you can see versus knowing there's a hairy furball of a mess of stuff to tackle somewhere.

✓ Having a system will boost your productivity and encourage you to prioritize.

✓ You will be less distracted and more present and mindful in the moment rather than mind full.

✓ You might even sleep better.

Tool #2: Get a Grip on Your Schedule

Is every day a "season of rush" for you? There's no question there are times in our year (or week or month) that can be more hectic than others. But for some people, the season of rush is every day. We live and work in a society that values productivity, and we do, do, do. But the frenzy of rushing can be tamed somewhat by being more conscious in how you schedule yourself. This isn't necessarily a natural habit for some people.

The Story at a Glance

A client I will call Maureen arrived to a phone-based coaching session extremely distracted. She had nearly forgotten about the scheduled appointment and wasn't prepared with an update or a focus for the call. I could hear the aura of rush when she arrived. After settling in a bit, she shared that she had just had a prior meeting with a prospective client and was disappointed with the outcome. She confessed that she had pretty much winged her new business meeting because she hadn't had time to adequately focus herself or do ample preparation before the meeting. Her schedule had been jam-packed with one meeting after another, and before she knew it, that important scheduled meeting had arrived. While she had hoped to have a few moments prior to the meeting to focus, she'd gotten stuck in traffic and had nearly been late.

Maureen is bright and capable, but her ad hoc approach to scheduling was frazzling her and derailing her success. Her stress was likely putting her brain in flight, or fright, inhibiting her ability to focus and be present (mindful) in her meeting. In our coaching call, I asked her several questions to explore how she generally scheduled herself and the impact some of her habits were having on her productivity, focus, and overall success. That conversation elicited some insights for Maureen. She recognized that she could make some small changes in her scheduling habits that would make big differences.

The Advice

Get a grip on your schedule, and check your habits. There are small changes you can make to ensure you have more control in your day and can be more productive, mindful, and focused in your activities and time.

Although we don't have complete control over our schedules (there are meetings scheduled on our behalf, obligations to fulfil, etc.), there is a lot we can do if we set the intention. Here are a few questions to help you assess your scheduling habits, along with some ideas to make this tool work for you.

Assess Your "Rushability" Quotient

- To what extent do you find yourself rushing to your meetings and appointments (on a scale of 1 to 10, with 10 being the highest)?

- Does your rush factor contribute to or sabotage your productivity, focus, and success? A little bit of pressure can sometimes work for us, as our brain likes a bit of stress, but too much can derail us. What is your sweet spot when it comes to scheduling your time?

- How much time do you leave in between meetings and appointments to shift gears, to get to your destination, and to allow for contingency if the meeting goes longer than expected? Can you squeeze a bit more margin between your scheduled meetings? How much margin would make a positive difference to you and be realistic for you to attain?

- How do you schedule time to think, plan, and reflect? What about simply getting your work done? Do any of these activities get scheduled, or do you try to squeeze them in after all the other meetings are done? How is that working for you?

- Where can you pay yourself first and schedule your time into the agenda? What difference would this make to your productivity, well-being, and overall success?

- How many others have access to your schedule? If your time is for the taking, how can you protect some time for priority work to ensure it's not snatched away?

- What is your relationship with white space in your agenda? Do you get any? Do you make sure you have some? Do you panic and fill it up?

Make It Work for You

Here are four scheduling tips to help you better manage your time.

1. **Build in more responsible margins of time.**
   Allow yourself time to get to meetings; account for common barriers (e.g., traffic); and focus and shift gears.

2. **Pay yourself first, and schedule yourself into your agenda.**
   Schedule time for essential tasks, such as planning, thinking, and working, and make sure your schedule is not only for official meetings with others. Also, use your schedule to commit time for essentials that are important to you outside of your work, such as exercise, family, and other meaningful pursuits.

3. **If you have an executive assistant, work with her or him to protect your time before people schedule themselves into it.**
   If others have access to your calendar, make sure you have already booked your key activities (even if they are not meetings) into your schedule to avoid a free-for-all on your time. If a meeting request is important enough, you can adjust accordingly.

4. **Don't be afraid of white space.**
   Think twice before you fill it all up. You might need it as the day wears on. It will never be wasted.

The Pay-Off

You will get a grip on your schedule and feel more in control of your time.

✓ You will minimize the constant rush factor and reduce your stress.
✓ You will be more prepared for your meetings.
✓ You will be more mindful, focused, and productive in the moment.
✓ You will have a greater sense of ownership of your time.

Tool #3: Prioritize and Triage

Prioritizing is an absolutely essential skill, especially as the volume of demands ramps up. Most of us know this intellectually, yet all too often, when in the throes of a busy, demanding time, we can forget this as we dive into our doing, doing, doing mode. We tend to not pay enough attention to the art of prioritizing, and this lack of prioritizing contributes to our feeling of chaos at having too much to do at once.

The Story at a Glance

A friend of mine, whom I will call Georgia, had been promoted and was tasked with building a new business unit within her organization. Her workload grew exponentially. While we were out for dinner one evening, she shared that she felt utterly bogged down. She was not yet fully staffed, but the incredible volume of work still had to get done. I asked her how she organized her load and what her key priorities were. She was tired, so her impulsive answer was "Everything is a priority!"

Really? Can you really fit forty-two hours in a twenty-four-hour day? Squeeze an elephant into a shoe? Stuff a boot into a buttonhole? You get the point.

Georgia actually is effective with her time and is a competent leader, but I share this anecdote as an example because many of us often feel this way. While in the moment, we lose sight of the need to prioritize or even triage. This is likely a classic example of the amygdala hijacking our brain. We know better, but our higher-thinking brain goes offline as we experience the moment of stress.

Choosing wisely what gets the attention first is a critical skill that we need to be able to call up at any given moment. When doing it all right now is simply not possible, we have to make choices by the minute, day, and week and throughout the continuum of our work and lives.

Priority.

Something given or meriting attention before competing alternatives[1]

The Advice

No matter how big or small a load might be—or how important the entire load is—it is always essential to prioritize. This gives you focus and a way of organizing. It also helps you set boundaries and know what can be shifted, reallocated, and rolled over. It also gives you a compass for when to use that essential phrase "No, not now."

And when there really is too much on your plate, prioritizing just won't cut it. It's time to triage, which is prioritizing on steroids! You must be even more ruthless with what gets reassigned, parked, or rolled over.

Make It Work for You

Prioritizing isn't a habit; it is a whole bunch of habits that you might need to call upon at any given time. Here are some ideas to develop your repertoire of prioritizing habits:

1. **Constantly ask this question: What is the priority right now/ today/this week?**
   Simply asking the question will remind you to focus on priorities. This is also a great question to bring your higher-thinking brain (the prefrontal cortex) back online and provide a sense of calm and order amid chaos. All too often, we reactively dive into "doing" mode before taking stock and evaluating if the task is the most important one to focus on at any given time. Or worse, we freeze and get stuck. This question can get you unstuck in any given moment.

2. **Distinguish different kinds of priorities.**
   Not all priorities are alike. For instance, some are important and time sensitive and need to be addressed immediately. Others are important and need some attention but are less time sensitive. However, if we leave those latter ones alone for too long, then sooner or later, they end up being urgent and important. Too many urgent and important

(time-sensitive) priorities contribute to that constant state of rushing and feeling overwhelmed. This can take us away from other important priorities and goals that give our work and lives meaning.

The late Stephen R. Covey identified a powerful framework for capturing and categorizing priorities in his bestselling book *The 7 Habits of Highly Effective People.*[2] He categorized by urgency and importance. See the quadrant below for examples. The key is to identify how you are allocating your time and gauge whether you are spending it wisely.

Time Management Matrix (Stephen R. Covey)

	Urgent	**Not Urgent**
Important	Activities: *Crises, pressing problems, deadline-driven projects, time-sensitive projects, etc.*	Activities: *Planning, prevention, relationship building, organizing, etc.*
Not Important	Activities: *Interruptions, some calls, some meetings, some emails, etc.*	Activities: *"Busy" nonessential work, time wasters, etc.*

Use this to identify, at any given time (day, week, month), how you are spending your time. Reflect on any changes that would make for a more productive, less rushed and less frenzied work life. And reflect on what other important (but less time-sensitive) priorities are getting left out and need to come to the fore.

3. **Ask, "What must be done? What would be nice to have done?"**
   These questions help distinguish priorities as well.

4. **Use priorities to establish boundaries, but maintain appropriate flexibility.**
   Having a sense of priorities for any given time frame helps set boundaries and gives you a compass for when to say no or "No, not

now." But it's also important to have some flexibility for unforeseen events or issues that need to be addressed (i.e., when to say yes). When these occur, learn how to roll over priorities. See the next point.

5. **Use the rollover strategy when needed.**
   Let's face it—plans and priorities are critical, but we can never fully foresee or control what will come our way on any given day. There will always be calls, emails, and issues we need to attend to that weren't on the planned priority list. That's where what I call the rollover strategy is useful. Rather than simply bumping off one activity to accommodate another, reflect on how rolling over a task will impact the next day (or other time frame). Rollovers are critical to good prioritizing skills.

6. **Account for time and energy.**
   One limitation associated with the grid described above is that urgency and importance do not cover another essential factor: energy and momentum. Sometimes taking a bit of time to get something off your plate that is quick and easy can have merit. Perhaps it will give you energy, knowing something is done, and create a sense of momentum (I will say more on action momentum in my discussion of another tool). So on occasion, those choices will trump in priority even if they aren't more urgent or important.

   For instance, if something comes to your attention (an email, a piece of mail, a request) and you can deal with it quickly, it might make sense to deal with it rather than add it onto a never-ending to-do list. The idea is to not lose substantial time or get distracted with multitudes of those kinds of tasks at the expense of the more pertinent priorities.

   You might want to label this particular list to reflect what it's all about. I like to call this the "Easy Sneezy—Get 'Er Done" list But hey, that's just me; you might have your own ideas.

The Pay-Off

Developing your prioritizing skills will give you more control over your time.

✓ Having clarity of your priorities will give you a compass for how to spend your limited resource of time and give you a reassuring road map when there's seemingly too much to do.

✓ An ongoing sense of priority will guide you towards better organization and purposeful productivity.

✓ Learning to say no and manage the loads will be easier when you have a clear sense of priorities and boundaries.

✓ You will feel more confident in how you navigate the continual chaos and recognize that not everything is urgent and important right now.

Tool #4: Manage Distractions

Have you ever had one of those days when you were all set to focus, focus, focus, and then …

"Oh, is that a butterfly on my windowsill?"

"I will just take this one call now before I get into my work."

"I'll take a few minutes to see who's on Facebook."

"Sure, I have a minute; come in and sit down, and we'll talk about your daughter's graduation-dress dilemma."

Oh yes. Distractions—they come in all shapes and sizes. And often, they are disguised as work, such as answering each call and email exactly when it comes in. Yes, that might be work, but is that what you need to focus on in that moment? Sometimes perhaps—but not always. When bogged down with too much to do and not enough time, recognizing distractions and learning to manage them is not only a good idea but also imperative.

The Story at a Glance

One of my clients—we'll refer to her as Connie—is a busy lawyer, and her struggle has been to stay on top of her workload and requisite billable hours. We've been working on her organizational skills, and she's made great progress. But one day, she came to a coaching call feeling rather frustrated. She was behind again and feeling bogged down.

She shared that she'd been doing a great job at prioritizing both in the broader view of her week and month as well as in her daily priorities. But all too often, she found she ran out of day and had to do too many task rollovers. I asked if she was putting unrealistic loads on her task list. Nope. She had learned that trap awhile ago, she told me. So what was eating up her day? I inquired.

She spoke about incoming calls from clients that sometimes kept her on the phone for much longer than necessary; walk-ins from colleagues to chat about matters that weren't necessarily urgent or time sensitive; and, finally, time spent surfing the web and reading that often extended well beyond reasonable breaks. She immediately attributed that third item as a distraction but didn't realize that the first two could be considered distractions as well until we explored further. Did these clients have time-sensitive, urgent issues? No, she said, and likewise for many of those conversations with her colleagues.

Ahhh, distractions—the eaters of time, snatchers of attention and focus. What to do?

The Advice

Getting a handle on your distractions is important as your work and life loads ramp up and your time is ever-more precious. In the face of feeling you have too much to do, learn what your distractions are and create strategies and structures to avoid the traps of unproductive time eaters.

Make It Work for You

- **Take stock of how you spend your time.**
  Often, our days are a blur. We know we did a bunch of stuff, but we might not have a clear idea of exactly how we are spending our time. Commit to keeping a time/task journal for at least a few days (ideally, a week). If you work in professional services where billing hours are part of your work life, you will be used to this. If not, it's worth a try. Even if you do work in a billable-time environment, it's important to note those lost hours that aren't attributable to work.

  Take note of everything you do. At the end of the week, review your list. Seeing this list in writing will reveal important information about how you spend your time.

  From this list, identify your distractions.

- **Label your activities.**
  It might be helpful to reflect on labels—such as the one identified in the grid I shared in the previous tool—that will illuminate those time eaters that might not be really important.

- **Discern between distractions caused by others and those that are self-imposed.**
  It will be helpful to identify the source of your distractions in order to create a response and strategy to minimize your distractions. Are you the main culprit? Perhaps some self-management will be in order. Or to what degree are others involved?

- **Manage the expectations of others.**
  In my client's example, she never set any expectations for how she would respond to client calls and emails. After exploring the impact of the time spent on ad hoc calls from her clients, she started to incorporate a policy where she committed to returning calls within a twenty-four-hour period or within the day for more urgent matters. She communicated this information to all her clients so that they would know when to expect a call back from her, and she reflected this in her outbound voicemail. Prior to doing this, she had felt obligated to pick up calls or return them immediately, even if they weren't urgent. While great customer service is important, her "jump when they call" habit detracted from her ability to provide truly great client service, because the distractions actually got in the way of getting her work done on behalf of clients. Reflect on your situation and identify where you can set boundaries and how best to communicate them.

- **Create systems for handling email.**
  Is the constant email *ting* a distraction for you from an energy and focus perspective? Some people find it helpful to have a routine and system where they check their emails at particular time intervals throughout the day. You decide what appropriate intervals might be.

- **For self-imposed distractions, take breaks, but set limits**. It's absolutely imperative to take breaks, and we'll deal with this topic in greater detail in a later section ("Clear the Cache"). But if you need a break, whether planned or spontaneous, be mindful of how much time you will allow yourself. In my client's situation, a short ten-minute break turned into more than an hour on too many occasions. Be mindful of the consequences, and own your time and choices.

The Pay-Off

Becoming more aware of your distractions will enable you to manage them better, resulting in more focus, productivity, and control over your most precious resources: time and attention.

- ✓ You will save time in the long run for what matters most.
- ✓ You will feel more in control of your time and able to focus more efficiently.
- ✓ Your brain will use less energy trying to deal with the chaos of constant interruptions.

Tool #5: Reign In the Multitasking

Check out a bunch of career ads these days, and count how often you see the word *multitasking* in the requisite skills. As complexity increases and competing demands and volumes of work soar, he or she who can multitask gets the job, keeps the job, and, well, keeps getting more stuff to do.

Work warriors wear their multitasking badges proudly. Then we take this skill home and multitask some more.

Multitasking is similar to how we felt about eating a lot of carbs in the early '90s. The more, the better, right?

Wrong!

Flying in the face of old notions, we're now learning that multitasking is, in fact, not the shiny attribute it's been touted to be all these years. While we do need skills to handle diverse demands in work and life, too much multitasking costs us precious energy, productivity, and even critical-thinking capacity.

Our brains aren't built for certain kinds of multitasking. Sure, we can walk and talk and eat and listen at the same time. But when we ask our brain to process unrelated information with multiple critical-thinking tasks at once, we actually compromise our short-term memory and cognitive-processing capacity.

In fact, what our brains do is switch from task to task—back and forth, back and forth. The faster we ask it to do so, the faster it switches. All this switching takes energy and amounts to wasted brain energy. This precious energy is not focused on thinking but, rather, is lost on switching.

Think of it like a driving a car. If you drive twenty miles (or kilometres) on the highway and then drive the same distance in the city, you will use more gas during the city drive. The constant stopping, turning, and shifting gears consumes more gas. The distance is the same, but the switching takes more energy.

Now put this analogy into the context of your day. If your entire day is filled with juggling tasks and little focused time, you will likely spend much more energy and feel more depleted than if you put the same amount of hours into your work with more focused time. And you might not be as sharp and effective, because you might compromise your brain's capacity to give you its best.

The Story at a Glance

Here's an embarrassing yet true story. I had just written part of a first draft of this chapter (without this story that I'm about to tell you). It was a Sunday, and I was getting ready to go to the gym but wanted to call a friend before I left so that I could share some news with her. I phoned her and, while chatting, decided to simultaneously pack my gym bag, change my clothes, and feed the cat. I must have come across like a moron, because she called me on it. As I was trying to relay a story to her, my focus was completely scattered, and I couldn't get a proper sentence out. I kept losing my train of thought. Not only did I forget key items to put in my gym bag, but I also couldn't communicate for the life of me. I was all over the place!

Realizing what I had just done gave me a great laugh, especially because I had just finished writing about the perils of multitasking! But the episode reinforced for me how much we have become ingrained in our so-called multitasking habit; we are always trying to jam in too many activities at once. This example was benign. But where else in our lives do we compromise our attention by attempting to do too many things at once?

I know, thankfully, in my coaching calls, I create a space and environment where I can completely focus my attention on the client. But at other times, when I'm doing other work, maybe I could do better.

How about you? Are you over-expressing that juggler tendency? Do you build in enough focus time? Are your thoughts fuzzy at times? Are you depleted at the end of the day?

Flow: The Sweetness of Focus Time

Our brains actually love to focus, and one of the rewards of focus can be an experience of flow. This is when you are in a zone where you lose yourself in an activity, and everything feels effortless and right. You feel completely on, and it is easy to lose your sense of time. Not only does this flow feel good in the moment, but it also provides a longer-lasting sense of gratification. Experts, such as Mihaly Csikszentmihalyi,[1] say flow is an essential ingredient to finding engagement and more joy and even success in our everyday work and lives. Csikszentmihalyi (pronounced "chick-sent-me-high"), a renowned psychologist and educator, has written extensively on the topic, including the book *Finding Flow*.[2]

The idea isn't to do less work per se but, rather, to find ways to focus our attention and build in more time for focused activity. And while our work might not offer the luxury of focusing for hours on end, there might be pockets of time we can carve out with intention.

The Advice

Take a timeout from your love affair with multitasking. Learn to tame the juggler in you and create more opportunities for focus time. Notice what happens to your productivity, energy, and overall sense of well-being. If you can't get enough flow time in your workday, try to include some in your after-work time.

Make It Work for You

- **Start small.**
  Don't expect to tame the multitasking habit overnight. Start small, and set aside short periods of time—even as little as twenty minutes— every day for a week for focused activity. Commit to putting your attention on one thing at a time—perhaps working on a particular project or completing a portion of it before moving on to another.

Then observe the impact that this focused time had on you. Were you more productive? Sharper and more creative? Did the time fly by? Was your energy increased or depleted?

You can then build up to longer periods as you see fit or are able to accommodate in your day (e.g., thirty minutes, forty minutes, etc.).

- **Support your intention with the right environment.**
  Turn off your phone, close your door, clear your desk—do anything that will give you the space and time to focus.

- **Schedule it.**
  Earlier, we talked about putting yourself into your own schedule for thinking time (see tool number two, "Get a Grip on Your Schedule"). Use this strategy to ensure you have focus time for important thinking activities. If you have a report to write or a plan to develop, block off time without other competing priorities and see how much more productive you will be. And as tool number four conveyed, beware of distractions that will impede your focus time.

- **Coach others to do the same**.
  If you are a leader, try to encourage others to set apart times to focus on a particular task. It sounds simple, but in our frenzied world of continuous rushing, focus time seems to be lost in the shuffle. You might notice a marked improvement in your own productivity as well as in that of your team.

The Pay-Off

Focus time will give you more energy and sharper thinking and will result in more productivity for your efforts.

- ✓ You will become more energy efficient with your time.
- ✓ You will experience more clarity in your thinking.
- ✓ You will enjoy a longer-lasting feeling of engagement that often results from flow and focus activities.
- ✓ You will experience more productivity and satisfaction in your day.

Tool #6: Learn to Say No

Are you addicted to the yes habit? "Addicted to yes" is a phrase I refer to when someone defaults to an automatic yes when there is a choice, and even a good reason, to say no. Work life is busy, and there is likely no shortage of requests to take on extra projects, join a volunteer committee, or chair the next fundraising event.

Saying yes to everything is unreasonable. Yet all too often, many of us respond reflexively and almost unconsciously from habit. Or we might be conscious of our yes habit, but we say yes begrudgingly. Our inner voices tell us that we must say yes or else there will be repercussions. We conjure up images of disapproval and disappointment; we don't want to rock the boat, so we agree in order to keep the peace. These inner voices, when unchecked, can drive our choices and actions in unproductive ways that don't serve us. Too much yes can lead to overload, fatigue, and suboptimal performance.

The Story at a Glance

A client I will refer to as Karla is quite an exceptional woman. She handles a large department of thirty; is a dedicated mother, a wife, and a friend to many; and also has a robust volunteer life. She is capable, smart, and generous. When I met her to explore coaching, one area that she felt she could use some help in was learning to say no. A prime example was related to her volunteer role at her church. Karla acknowledged that her contribution was valued and appreciated, but the requests for support were starting to become more than she had bargained for. She wanted to say no to some of the requests but didn't know how—and she felt bad about saying no. So instead, she started to avoid going to church. The avoidance strategy wasn't working. Not only was she missing her church experience, but she was also still getting requests via email and phone.

When I asked her what stopped her from saying no to some of those requests, Karla explained she felt guilty doing that and wondered if she'd be disappointing people. She also didn't know quite how to say no without compromising the relationship.

Karla had some limiting beliefs related to saying no. Her automatic yes habit was compromising her emotional well-being. In a nutshell, by not saying no when it mattered, Karla's volunteer role was becoming a good thing gone bad.

We worked together on this issue, and Karla said learning when and how to say no was one of the most powerful lessons of our time together. This new ability gave her confidence to assert herself in many situations beyond the church and allowed her the freedom to create a better balance with her work, volunteer life, and personal pursuits.

The Advice

Learn to manage your reflexive yes habit, and say no when it counts.

Saying no is difficult for many people. But often, the roadblock starts with oneself. Once we recognize our limiting beliefs, we can then more appropriately say no when it matters. It is also important to learn how to appropriately say no.

Make It Work for You

- **Discern and challenge your limiting beliefs.**
  Become aware of the internal conversations and thoughts that prompt you to say yes. Do you feel guilty saying no? Do you fear you will damage the relationship or be thought less of? Are there other reasons? Listen in to the dialogue your inner voice is having. Then assess which of your beliefs are valid and which can be considered limiting beliefs. For instance, thoughts such as *I am wrong for saying no; they will like me less* might be limiting beliefs. However, thoughts such as *I want to say no but don't know quite how to say it* are valid obstacles that you can overcome by learning some helpful communications skills.

- **Determine your boundaries.**
  It will be hard to say no to others unless you are clear on your priorities and boundaries. For example, you might have established a priority

to spend a certain amount of time with your family, and a boundary might be an amount of time that you are willing to give to a particular pursuit. Once you've established and validated with yourself your priorities and boundaries, use them as an internal compass to help you determine when to say no on a case-by-case basis.

- **Recognize your triggers.**
  Sometimes it is easy to say no to certain people and situations and more difficult with others. Learn to notice your personal triggers so that you can self-manage those times you are most apt to go into a yes autopilot mode.

- **Pause when necessary.**
  Learn to pause before automatically saying yes. Buy yourself a few moments to collect your thoughts (e.g., "Let me get back to you in a few moments," or another appropriate time frame).

- **Learn how to appropriately convey no.**
  Once you've broken the habit of automatically saying yes, it is also important to learn how to say no appropriately. Here are a few tips on how to say no.

  - **Acknowledge the request before you say no:** *"Thank you for inviting me to this opportunity. I appreciate this offer to join the committee, but I can't at this time because ..."*

  - **Share your reason, and speak from a voice of responsibility when appropriate:** *"I would like to help on this project, but if I took this on, I would be jeopardizing my other work priorities as per my other committed projects."*

  - **Make another offer that is doable for you:** *"While I can't take this project on at this time, I'd be happy to offer you a few ideas and thoughts that may be useful or suggest some other people you might want to approach."*

- **Show empathy:** *"I get that this is important to you and that you are in a tough spot, but I'm not in a good position to take this on right now."*

- **Be dependable:** *"I would take this on only if I knew I could do the work to the standard you need. At this time, I wouldn't be able to give the necessary time or focus, so I'd rather be honest with you up front."*

- **Practise.**
  Learning to say no is an assertiveness skill and part of the spectrum of emotionally intelligent competencies. It might take a bit of practice. In the next week, notice those situations that call for a no, and see if you can catch yourself in the moment before you say yes automatically. Practise the exercises as per the instructions above, and afterwards, reflect and ask yourself the following questions: How did that go? What did I do well? What can I improve? What was the reaction? How much of the initial reactive angst was my own worrying versus genuine issues? What did I learn?

  Over time, you will notice a new habit emerge—one where you can appropriately assert yourself and say no with confidence, empathy, and diplomacy.

The Pay-Off

Learning to say no at the appropriate time is an emotionally intelligent way to handle overload.

✓ You will manage your workload and avoid the risk of taking on more than you can handle.
✓ You will maintain good relationships without having to be a yes person.
✓ You will earn the respect of others, as saying no when it is appropriate gives others confidence in your ability to determine your limits.
✓ You will increase your confidence; learning to say no can boost your efficacy and leadership.

Tool #7: Manage the Paradox of Choice at the Buffet of Life

As we explore this concept of overwhelm, it is easy to assume that our overload can exclusively be attributed to all the external demands and obligations that others put upon us. But that would be inaccurate. Often, we are the culprits of our own overload, particularly in the case of people who like to engage full out in life both in their discretionary choices and their professional and personal pursuits. There are a lot of enticements in the buffet of life, and for some of us, gorging gets us into trouble. The opposite—not engaging enough—is equally unhealthy for our well-being. Reflect on your own style: Are you a gorger or a nibbler or somewhere in between?

The Story at a Glance

Confession: I am a gorger at the buffet of life! I know that I have a tendency to take on large loads in both work and play, and all too often, a great part of my experience of overload is because I have chosen to do too much. I've signed up for too many courses (but they are all great, and I really want to do them!); I've taken on too many big projects, such as this book (come on—how can I not write this book?); I am a member of a book club (reading is important, no?); I get to the gym for my boot camp, Pilates, and stretching classes (physical well-being is essential to my overall well-being plan); and so on.

Oh yes, I want to do it all, and it all matters to me. But I know I've passed the tipping point of engagement when I find myself wading in the overwhelm swamp. Oh, where's the joy?

The Advice

As a go-getter myself, I'm not going to tell you to cut back here or there. But this is what I will advise: Be aware of and take responsibility for the choices you are making at the buffet of work and life. Check in frequently, and ask yourself if your choices are contributing to your well-being or impeding it. Do the benefits of your activities outweigh occasional feelings of overload, or has the tipping point leaned towards too much overwhelm, leaving you with more stress than joy? If your answer leans towards the latter, it's time to make some changes.

Make It Work for You

If you are like me, simply asking you to choose less will be challenging. But perhaps there are better ways to approach the buffet of life—to enjoy it and sidestep the overwhelm swamp. Here are some ideas.

- **If you like variety in your life, choose smaller portions for particular pursuits.**

  For instance, golf is one of my summer activities, but I have learned (after many frustrating years) that given all my other pursuits, golfing two to three times a week is not always reasonable. So golf these days is now a delightful side dish rather than an entrée in my summer pursuits. I manage to get out frequently enough and leave room for the other things I enjoy doing.

- **Manage your own expectations.**

  Using the golf example above, in past years, I would set up an expectation that "This will be the year that I will get out earlier, golf more often, go to the range, and become a real golfer." I'd experience frustration when that didn't happen, and I judged myself. Crazy, eh? Once I became aware of what I was doing to myself, I realized how insane that behaviour was. Golf wasn't—and had never been—a huge priority for me, but I was setting standards for myself as if it were. So I reset my expectations to align more realistically with my more meaningful goals and priorities. Now I play as little (or frequently) as I like—without the frustration of feeling as if it is not enough.

Golf is just one example from my life. Think about your life and the activities you are committing to. Where are you setting standards and expectations that need to be readjusted to more accurately reflect your true priorities?

- **Choose the right balance of activities**.
  Often, go-getters go get 'em with such gusto that we can sabotage our own balance with our overzealous ambitions.

  It's important to have a portfolio of activities that provides a healthy balance. Are all your activities calling on you to excel, work, drive, and push? Are there enough activities in your life that allow you to rest, refresh, and simply be? Which choices nourish you, and which deplete you? There's no one-size-fits-all recipe, but regularly check in by asking yourself, "Is this the right balance of choices right now?" See chapter 6 (tool number fifteen) for thoughts on creating a happiness portfolio.

- **Adjust accordingly**.
  Work and life are dynamic and fluid. We need to adjust constantly to accommodate the demands. Some days, weeks, and seasons allow us to do more of certain activities, and other times allow less time for those pursuits. Recognize this, and adjust your portfolio of activities accordingly. This will help keep you from trying to maintain a fixed approach to balance. Balance needs to ebb and flow with the realities and demands of life.

- **(Bonus tip) Start an "Oh bleep! Another idea!" file**.
  This tip is for you if you are creative and constantly coming up with new ideas and perhaps also have a passion for shiny new things (to learn, to do, etc.). These are not bad qualities. That said, having a lot of passion, creativity, and diverse interests can sometimes put a pinch on that focus thing we talked about earlier—and on your time. In my experience, I've learned to not completely squelch my ideas and interests but to find a way to park them until there is a better time. To do this, I have created an "Oh bleep! Another idea!" file. I put a lot of great ideas in there, and when the time is right, I revisit them and bring them back out. I've offered this tip to many others who share similar challenges, and they love it. Try it out, and see if it helps you manage the tendency towards overextending yourself without compromising your passion and creativity.

The Pay-Off

Becoming aware of your choices and taking responsibility for what you choose will help you in a myriad of ways.

- ✓ You will manage your load and avoid taking on too much.
- ✓ You will learn to create balance in the ebb and flow of life.
- ✓ You will become aware of what's really important to you, and then you can make choices accordingly.
- ✓ You will find ways to keep your passion alive without compromising your sanity.

Chapter 5
Mindful: Develop Conscious
and Empowering Mindsets

Managing your mindset is critical when dealing with overload. Remember this question: "Is that a lion, a tiger, or just a tight deadline and demanding boss?" Your interpretation and perception will impact your reaction, frame of mind, mood, and even physical and biological responses.

Is your immediate interpretation accurate and always representing the ultimate truth? Of course not! We've all heard the expression "Perception is reality," and if that is true, then there can be more than one possible reality. Your mindset will determine whether you trigger the limbic system with an amygdala attack or maximize the potential of your prefrontal cortex (a.k.a. higher-thinking brain) to do its good work.

Being mindful of our reactive ways of thinking and trying out new ways of more consciously and intentionally looking at a situation is what this section is all about.

Identify the thoughts that limit you, and trade up for better ones. Challenging your perceptions to shift how you experience life is the work of emotional intelligence.

Here's a glimpse of the strategies we will explore in this part of the toolkit. They will help you challenge your reactive and limiting thoughts and shift your perception to a more reflective, empowering, and conscious mindset—and often in just a moment's time.

Tools → Develop Conscious and Empowering Mindsets

8. Tame the Inner Critics
9. Climb Your Mountains One Step at a Time
10. Ask, "What *Can* I Do Now?"
11. Use Powerful Questions: The New Swiss Army Knife
12. Pause, Park, Reflect: The Power of Journaling
13. Clear the Cache

Tool #8: Tame the Inner Critics

We all have inner critics.[1] The inner critic is a negative voice (or series of voices) within us that exaggerates our doubts and questions our abilities beyond reason. The inner critic, also sometimes referred to as a gremlin, saboteur, or voice of judgment, speaks from the voice of fear, limiting beliefs, negative judgment, and exaggeration. The main work of our inner critic is to keep us stuck, small, and doing less than we are capable of. The inner critic hates change and does not like to see us grow. Inner critics usually come out to play when they sniff the risk of possibility or, worse, greatness.

The higher-thinking brain (the prefrontal cortex) does not like it when we feel fearful, nor does it like the feeling of threat to our egos (i.e., the possibility of looking bad). The inner critic can trigger your brain's limbic system, fire up the amygdala and bring the alarms!

The Story at a Glance

"I will never get through this work. This is going to be a disaster. I will look bad. This is too much for me. I will disappoint others if I say no. I am an impostor. I can't. I can't. I can't!"

Sound familiar? This story belongs to all of us. We've all had those internal conversations. Those words are usually the voices and stories of inner critics. Sometimes they show up in our actual words. Other times, they lurk in our subconscious, and we aren't even aware that they are influencing our feelings, beliefs, and actions.

While everyone has inner critics, what distinguishes those who are most masterful and successful in their lives is their ability to recognize and manage their inner critics. They also learn to identify the triggers that tend to prompt their inner critics to show up.

One of my clients, Marilyn, was deep into BMW mode in one of our coaching calls. When I say BMW, I'm not referring to a car. In my world, *BMW* stands for "bitch, moan, and whine." She was going on and on about how she had no time; was going to fail, crash, and burn on her work project; and was at the end of her rope. Because I knew Marilyn quite well, I realized she was having a gremlin, or inner critic, moment. She was tired, and this is when our inner critics often come out to haunt us, because we are vulnerable. Having worked on her inner-critic awareness skills already, I simply asked, "So now that we have heard from your inner critic, what might the rest of you have to say?"

Marilyn stopped in her tracks and let out a huge belly laugh. She realized immediately that she had let her inner critics take over and that they were driving the show. Recognizing this, she shifted gears and went on to name her other voices and tap into what they would say:

"Well, my voice of trust says I've done this before and can do this too. My voice of reason says if I triage a little bit and focus on the most important part first—the plan and strategy—the rest will be a lot easier. My voice of action says if I can just get started, I will feel better." And she went on with more of this kind of conversation.

This kind of thinking and dialogue immediately shifted Marilyn away from the (perceived) territory of danger and moved her towards an instant feeling of calm, confidence, and clarity. In biological terms, Marilyn's mindset shift brought a chemical response that doused the fires of the stress response. She traded the alarm/stress chemicals (cortisol and adrenaline) for the calming hormone (GABA). This process is akin to taking an antacid for the brain—giving some immediate relief and making room for better thinking.

Within just a few moments, Marilyn was feeling much more able to tackle her load. A few months prior, Marilyn would not necessarily have been able to transition so quickly to this more empowered mindset. In our time together, she had learned strategies for doing this and had been developing her muscle (a.k.a. a habit for more-empowered thinking), so with just a small nudge from me, she was able to tap into her more resourceful self.

This skill is one of the most important in the emotional intelligence toolbox. Learning to self-manage our limiting perspectives and shift into a more resourceful state of mind is integral to managing overwhelm and, just as importantly, overall well-being.

The Advice

Get to know your inner critics that embody limiting beliefs. Learn to manage them. Know your triggers. Become masterful at self-observation so that you can recognize those inner-critic moments and transition to your resourceful, reasonable self.

Make It Work for You

This is not a one-time tool. We never get completely rid of our inner critics. We have to stay mindful throughout our life. Each of us will have our own unique voices of doubt. Some of us even have a team of inner critics (I call mine my "board"). This is not a bad thing. Do not judge yourself for having inner critics. It's part of being human. Instead, acknowledge yourself for recognizing your inner critics and commit to noticing them and managing them when they show up.

Here's a process to help you get acquainted with your inner critics and learn to manage them in the moment.

Step #1: Meet Your Inner Critics

You can't manage your inner critics unless you are aware of them and can observe them when they show up. It's also important to recognize the negative impact they have on you so that you can realize that rather than serving you, they are keeping you unreasonably small, doubtful, and stuck. Simply stay tuned in to yourself, and at any given moment when you are feeling less resourceful and confident, ask yourself if there is an inner critic at play.

To assess if your fears or doubts are legitimate, take the evidence test. Ask yourself if your fears, doubts, and worries are justified or exaggerated. If they are perfectly justified, then this voice might not be an inner critic. Perhaps there is something you need to deal with. Keep in mind that it is fine to have reasonable fear about something. The distinction is that the inner critic will magnify your fears, doubts, and judgments to the point that they no longer serve you.

Step #2: Name Your Inner Critics and Give Them a Shape

Putting a face, name, and structure to your inner critics makes it easier to notice and distinguish them when they show up. This leverages the wonderful work of the right brain. Our right-brain hemisphere loves metaphors and visuals. Having a visual in your mind can give you quick access to observing your limiting belief when it shows up.

If you are game, take out scissors, markers, magazines, or anything that inspires your creativity. Draw, define, and create a picture of your inner critic. If you are not inclined to go the fully creative route, simply write up a description and try to picture it in your mind.

Answer these questions to help put shape to your inner critic: What is its name? What does it look like? How does it feel in your body? What words, phrases, and sounds does it make (it always has something to say—get to know its dialogue)? What's the tone?

This activity is meant to be done in a playful spirit. No judging here! That would be an inner critic doing the judging. The intent of this exercise is to make it easier to distinguish these limiting forces within as separate from your authentic, trusting, wise, and reasonable self.

Step #3: Start the Noticing Game

Now that you are distinguishing some of your critics, the next step is to simply notice when they show up at any given moment. This is a lifelong game, but you'll want to put more attention on the early days of getting to know your critics.

To be able to notice an inner critic at any given time (particularly when in a moment of doubt or stress), you will need to develop an intentional mindset to observe yourself. If you catch yourself feeling particularly worried, uncomfortable, stressed, or tense, chances are, an inner critic is involved.

Take a moment to reflect and ask yourself a few questions to help you see your inner critic: What's going on here? What am I thinking and feeling, and whose voice is this (the voice of an inner critic or my voice of reason)? What is it saying? Is it justified or exaggerated? What's the impact of these limiting beliefs on me?

Notice what happens when you ask these questions and start to recognize your inner critics. These questions bring the prefrontal cortex back online and can immediately bring a dose of calm and clarity to help you further distinguish what's real and what's not.

The next step is to intentionally call up other parts of yourself, such as your voice of reason.

Step #4: Choose to Listen to Your Other More Empowered Voices

The next step is to intentionally nudge yourself towards a more empowered and truthful state. We have an infinite number of resources to tap into. It's helpful to simply ask yourself a question such as the following: "What does my voice of reason have to say?" Or ask to hear from your voice of trust, empowerment, past experience, wisdom, etc. The idea is to deliberately call upon other parts of yourself that are distinct from your inner critics and more inclined to support you rather than obstruct you.

And because the right-brain hemisphere loves images and metaphors, it can also be helpful to visualize yourself putting the inner critic somewhere that quiets the disruptive voices.

Bonus Step #5: Recognize Your Triggers

Over time, you will become more masterful at recognizing your inner critics in the moment. Knowing your triggers will enable you to anticipate inner-critic moments and pre-empt them with deliberate, empowering strategies.

The Pay-Off

Recognizing your limiting mindset is the first and most critical step in accessing a more empowering mindset.

✓ You will have a powerful tool at your disposal at any given time to manage self-doubts and access your resourceful, capable, and wise self.
✓ Learning to minimize unproductive, self-limiting beliefs will free up more of your whole, creative, and resourceful self to tackle the opportunities, challenges, and loads of the day.
✓ You will have more energy in the reserve without having to work against the depleting forces of inner critics.

Tool #9: Climb Your Mountains One Step at a Time

I think that now and again, we can all claim to have been daunted by a particular task. Sometimes these tasks truly are mountainous, and other times, they might only appear to be so. Whether you are making a mountain out of a molehill or are truly confronted by a big, hairy, giant mound of a task, it's not uncommon to occasionally feel overwhelmed in light of everything else on your plate. A common response to this is to ignore the task for a while. Yes, you read that correctly: procrastination is a common response, but it is certainly not an effective one! Procrastination, my friends, can add substantially to that heaviness in our hearts and contribute to our sense of burden.

The Story at a Glance

I was out walking one evening with a good friend of mine, Marcy, whom I've known for more than forty years (yes, this is her real name!). I know Marcy to be an exceptionally capable woman. She has a full family life, juggles a big job at a bank, and somehow always manages to keep it all together. But on this evening, she vented that she was feeling befuddled by the planning of her son's bar mitzvah. She confessed she had done nothing and was worried because time was ticking away. But she was in "Stucksville." "What's up with that?" I asked. She didn't know—or so she said.

I then had a hunch she was thinking about the whole mound of stuff that needed to get done and, in her mind, was trying to untangle a nasty furball of to-dos all at once. No wonder she was in distress!

So I asked, "What's the first thing that needs to get done?"

She said, "I have to book a location."

I asked if she had any ideas, and she said she did. I asked if it would be helpful if she had that sorted out. She thought it would. "What is the first thing you need to do?" I asked.

She said she had to make a few calls.

"What is stopping you from making some calls?"

"Nothing really," she said.

So I asked the most obvious question: "When will you make those calls?"

She said the next morning. And then we both laughed because that discussion had taken about a minute and a half, yet she said it felt as if a hundred-pound load had been lifted off her chest.

Yeah, it was that easy. (I warned you some of these ideas would be embarrassingly simple!)

The rest is history. From there, she was to tackle one piece of this seemingly mountainous project at a time, and ta-da! She got it all done, and it was a beautiful celebratory event. She had needed the nudge to start the climb up the mountain by focusing on the first steps. After scaling that first part of the climb, she had experienced a sense of accomplishment, and the next part of the climb had felt easier. This is what is referred to as action momentum.

Sometimes all we need to focus on is getting started. Being in action—even if beginning with just one small starting step—can help create a sense of momentum that will empower us to take the next step and the one after it and so on.

But there might be another explanation. Recall the Zeigarnik effect introduced earlier with the first tool ("Get It out of Your Head"), which describes a state where our minds get fixated on unfinished business. I wonder if in starting a project, we are more likely to feel the pull towards completing it if it's a meaningful goal. Just a thought.

The Advice

Step back from the mountain (project, task, etc.) that is keeping you stuck. Ask if you are aiming for the top of the mountain or setting your sights on the first or immediate next leg of the journey. Take some time to focus on a starting plan, and most importantly, break the challenge down into manageable parts.

Remember the adage that a journey starts with a single step. Mountain climbers know this, and they scale their mountains one stage at a time. They plan the climb with milestones along the way. This approach is what's needed for our own mountains.

Make It Work for You

Take a look at a project that you feel is mountainous to you. Then try these steps:

1. Set your sights on a way to start. It might be at the beginning, or it might be somewhere that provides an easy entry. It doesn't matter. Simply start.
2. Break the mountain into smaller, more doable chunks.
3. Create a plan so that you can see the steps instead of trying to take in the entire task at once.
4. Identify the first milestone, and focus your attention on that part of the mountain.
5. Move into action with that first step, and experience action momentum.
6. Keep moving one step (milestone, chunk) at a time.
7. Remember that small steps add up to a solid journey.
8. Celebrate success along the way.

This tool seems obvious, but like many of the other simple strategies, it goes out of our mindset when we are overwhelmed. Find a way to create a reminder for yourself next time you are faced with a mountain of a task.

The Pay-Off

Remembering to scale your mountains in smaller steps can help you deal with large, complex, and seemingly overwhelming tasks.

- ✓ Breaking your mountain (or perceived mountain) into manageable chunks will reduce brain and mind overwhelm.
- ✓ Getting started provides a sense of action momentum, making the next parts easier.
- ✓ Breaking large tasks into smaller parts provides opportunities for a sense of completion and reduces the perception of the never-ending task list.
- ✓ The brain loves a plan! You will be rewarded with a sense of greater ease, focus, and peace of mind.

Tool #10: Ask, "What *Can* I Do Now?"

So you've practised many of the strategies in your toolbox, such as chunking down your mountains into smaller-sized tasks, and you've done your best to organize yourself so that you are more in control of your schedule and workload. And you know the difference between your inner critic and your voice of reason.

And yet, oh dear, you still find yourself in a moment of Stucksville and frustration. Oh, what to do?

The Story at a Glance
We all have those moments of feeling stuck.

I certainly have had my share, even as recently as writing this book. In the fall of 2012, I was in the midst of my busiest work season of the year. Without diving into all the details, let's just say that one week was particularly frenzied, and I felt overloaded, to say the least. I had queued up some time to work on my book, but trying to write was a nonstarter that day. I couldn't get a proper thought out, and worse, my frustration was compounded by a feeling that I didn't have enough time to put in the effort and writing time I felt I needed to move this project forward.

But thankfully, I recognize when I am in that mindset and have tools to draw on. The key is to choose the right tool at the right time. I knew I needed two things: first, to be in action to get out of my moment of "brain stuck" (in this case, writer's block), and second, to alleviate the frustration of not having enough time to do more.

So I went to one of my favourite *big* little ideas that always serves me well. Like many of the other ideas presented, this is incredibly simple yet works powerfully.

I simply asked myself, "What *can* I do now?"

The minute I brought that question into my consciousness, I immediately shifted into a more productive and more abundant state. Rather than focusing on what I couldn't tackle (for all the various reasons), I chose bits that I *could* do right now. This gave me a sense of empowerment and control and put me into action momentum. Bit by bit, this appreciative approach of focusing on what I *could* do defrosted my brain freeze, enabling me to carry on. It also relieved me of the burden of feeling that I was not doing enough.

This type of question completely refocuses the brain on possibility and away from the perspectives of impossibility, limitations, and chaos. It also brings you into the present and gives you a sense of some control and choice in the *now*. This is a brain-friendly benefit because one of the conditions for optimizing the prefrontal cortex is to feel we have choice and empowerment. When those elements are threatened, our PFC (prefrontal cortex) functions become compromised.

In some ways, this idea is similar to the strategy of chunking down large tasks in the previous tool ("Climb Your Mountains") because it helps get you started. But this particular tool also has the benefit of freeing you from the feeling of constraint or limitation that creates a threat signal to the brain. Rather than shutting down your brain, you feel an expansion of possibility and resourcefulness.

Sometimes we need to hold particular questions in a special place because we can use them over and over again; they warrant the title of "powerful questions"—or "power tools," in my vocabulary.

"What *can* I do now?" is that kind of question.

Kudos for this powerfully worded question goes to Kim George,[1] a fellow coach, author of *Coaching into Greatness*,[2] and founder of the Abundance Intelligence Institute[.3] Kim put a luminous spotlight on this question in her work on Abundance Intelligence˚. I participated in one of her advanced coach-training programs many years ago, and among other gems, I found this particular question extraordinarily useful.

Kim says this question is framed from an abundant mindset. Conversely, when we are feeling stuck and frustrated, we are likely operating from a scarcity mindset, where we default to a limiting perspective that focuses on what we *can't* do and all the reasons why we *can't* do something.

The Advice

Keep this question close by at all times, and when feeling stuck, frustrated, or as if you do not have enough time or resources, ask, "What *can* I do?"

Make It Work for You

- **Develop a structure for remembering this question.**
  It's easy to forget which question to ask when we are in a tailspin of doubt, fear, and other limiting beliefs. So find a way to keep this question (and any others you find particularly useful) accessible so that you can draw on it at any given moment. Perhaps you can create a poster, photo, illustration, or quote in your work area (remember how the right brain loves visuals and metaphors) or a daily reminder in your calendar when you know you will be under big loads.

- **When work and life are extraordinarily hectic and time is seemingly scarce, create a practice of asking this question daily.**
  Whether you ask this at the beginning of the day or at some other time during the day, create the intention of asking it regularly so that it becomes more automatic and easily accessible than its counterpart ("Why can't I ...?"). Repetitive practice creates new neuropaths in the brain, and eventually, asking this question will become more of a habit.

The next tool will expand on the power of questions. Any question that opens you up to greater possibility is a good question. This one—"What *can* you do now?"—just happens to be one of my favourites!

The Pay-Off

When you feel stuck or frustrated with constrained time, asking this simple question can be the lever to get you unstuck and open up your heart, brain, and mind.

✓ You will be able to focus your mind on the present and on possibility.
✓ You will know you can right-size your actions for the situation, and you will have a sense of efficacy and accomplishment.
✓ You will reduce the brain threat associated with feeling as if you have no control and will put yourself back on the path to empowerment.
✓ You will experience self-trust, respecting your capacity for that moment in time.

Tool #11: Use Powerful Questions: The New Swiss Army Knife

If you reflect on the previous tools presented so far, you will notice they all have something in common: questions. What *can* I do now? What are my priorities? What can I say no to? What does my voice of trust say? And so on.

Learning to ask the right question of yourself and others is one of the most important skills you can have in your professional and personal toolbox. The right question can open up doors to new thinking, more choices, a more empowered mindset, the expansion of ideas and creativity, better relationships, deeper self-trust and confidence, more clarity, and much more.

And just as importantly, asking the right kinds of questions can bring your prefrontal cortex back online and boost your higher-thinking capacity. The right question can shift us away from the perception of limits, danger, or risk and instead reframe our mindset towards opportunity, resourcefulness, and possibility—all conditions the higher-thinking brain likes and needs to do its job at an optimal level.

Powerful questions[1] can create this state and are so versatile that we can consider them the Swiss army knife of tools. You don't want to leave home without them!

The Story at a Glance

In my experience coaching hundreds of people over the years, I have observed that virtually every shift, commitment, or insight a client experiences from coaching stems from at least one question, if not many. A few examples follow (names have been changed).

"What do you want?" got Mary to hone in on her specific goals in preparation for a tough conversation at work.

73

"How will you know?" got Jim to establish some criteria for success for a goal that had been vague for too long.

"What's at stake?" got Solange to get to the heart of the matter and clarify why she was perturbed by a turn of events in her work life.

"What will you do?" got Marc into action and commitment.

"How will you stay accountable?" got Mel to create structures to keep her true to her commitment.

You don't have to be a coach to ask good questions. In fact, everyone can benefit from learning this skill.

Marilee Adams,[2] founder of the Inquiry Institute[3] and author of *Change Your Questions, Change Your Life*,[4] says, "A question not asked is a door not opened."

At the same time, this skill is not about asking *any* question but, rather, about learning to ask the right kind of question for the situation. Good questions come from an open, curious, learner mindset. Conversely, questions that come from what Marilee Adams calls a judger orientation[5] can debilitate us. *Why can't I get this right? What's wrong with him/me/them?* Questions from the judger mindset limit our possibilities and can actually perpetuate our sense of being stuck and frustrated.

Note the distinction: a question anchored in critical-thinking skills and using your good judgment (from experience, intuition, etc.) is not the same as what we describe as the judger mindset. The latter type of questioning is the nonproductive kind; the former is appropriate if framed in the learner mindset.

The Advice
Develop the habit and the art of asking open, learner-oriented questions of yourself and others.

Make It Work for You

There is an infinite list of questions that can serve at any given moment. Here are some ideas to build your question-thinking mindset.

- **Be alert and listen for good questions.**
  Noticing others ask effective questions can help reinforce the skill of asking powerful questions.

- **Practise, practise, practise—with yourself and with others.**
  Wire the brain to develop the habit of asking open, learner-oriented questions.

- **Remember that good questions need not be complex.**
  A question such as "What else is possible?" can be the right question when trying to come up with new solutions. Or "What do I want?" can help give you clarity on your objectives in a situation.

- **Be curious!**
  Curiosity is an essential skill in asking a learner-oriented question.

- **Practise brainstorming questions before you brainstorm answers.**
  Marilee Adams says before diving into solution-finding, first try to come up with good questions, because the right question might expand your thinking and help you reach better solutions.

- **Develop a bank of questions that you can draw on from time to time, and include questions that are reusable.**
  For instance, you might identify a few of your favourite questions that will be of value on a regular basis. "What *can* you do now?" is a good example of this kind of question (see the previous tool for more on this point).

Here are a few examples to get you started on your bank of questions. Rather than creating a random list, categorize the questions to help with different purposes.

Finding new solutions:
What else can you do?
What have you not thought of yet?
What is one more idea that builds on this idea?
Come up with your own _____

Dealing with a sense of too much to do:
Where can I better organize myself?
Who can I ask for support?
What are my priorities right now?
What can I let go of, say no to, or reschedule?
Come up with your own _____

Building self-trust and confidence:
Which of my strengths can I tap into to get through this?
What from my past experience can I draw from?
What would my voice of courage and self-trust say?
Come up with your own _____

Building understanding in relationships:
What are they wanting?
What are they thinking?
How can we make this a win-win situation?
Come up with your own _____

Getting into learner mode:
What's the right question to ask now?
If I were truly standing in curiosity right now, what would I want to ask?
What is a learner's way of looking at this situation?
Come up with your own _____

Boosting your mood (I will further discuss these in the "Mind Your Mood" section):
What am I grateful for?
What went well?
What am I looking forward to?
Come up with your own _____

The Pay-Off

Learning to ask the right questions in the right situation and moment can vastly shift your perspective and put your brain and mind into a more resourceful and creative state.

✓ You will open new doors to new thinking and new ideas.
✓ Good questions help you organize and focus your thoughts when you need it most.
✓ You will be in a calmer, more confident, and more peaceful state of mind.
✓ Effective questions give access to your wisdom, creativity, self-trust, compassion, and more.

Tool #12: Pause, Park, Reflect: The Power of Journaling

As I mentioned earlier, the season of rush is now year-long. In our busyness, we often default to rush-and-react mode when what we really need is a reflective mindset to better navigate the demands of work and life. If you recall, this section of your toolkit emphasizes the need to be more conscious of your reactive and sometimes limiting thoughts and trade up for more productive, empowering mindsets. Journaling gives you the structure to pause, park, reflect, and then appropriately respond.

But is there enough time to reflect in our jam-packed lives? Yes, there is. Journaling does not have to take a lot of time. Sometimes it takes only a few moments. Yet the benefits are substantial.

Reflective journaling helps you learn about yourself and take a thoughtful approach in responding to any given situation. A written journal captures and deepens your learning; builds on insights; furthers your development; and helps you hold yourself accountable for your mindset, attitudes, and actions. Journaling makes your learning more tangible and longer lasting. Reflective inquiry through journaling develops an active learner's mindset, which is imperative in developing a more conscious mindset.

And finally, from a brain-smart perspective, journaling can slow down your fast-thinking reactions and help you tame your brain when confronted by a potential stress trigger.

I encourage my clients to journal as part of their coaching programs, and many have said the journaling greatly deepened and expanded their learning and their transformative experiences well beyond the coaching conversations.

The Story at a Glance

I have been journaling for more than thirty years. My eighth-grade creative-writing teacher introduced the class to journaling and it was mandatory. It was awkward in those days, and I never quite knew what to write about. But I stuck with it, and years later, my journaling took on a life of its own. In the early days, I did a lot of "here's what I did today" entries as well as BMW journaling (BMW as in "bitch, moan, and whine"). Those entries had merit, because sometimes you just have to vent. But in later years, I learned the power of journaling with intention and focused inquiry. Today, I can't live without this incredible tool. Journaling helps me work out issues on my mind, get clarity and peace of mind, and make better decisions. I also use journaling to capture and savour the good moments and great stuff occurring. Celebratory journaling is a powerful mood-boosting exercise (more about this in the next section, which focuses on positivity). When life is chaotic, my journaling anchors me by helping me to focus on what's going well and what I need to prioritize.

The Advice

Try keeping a journal. Becoming a reflective leader in your work and personal life is not a one-shot deal. It needs to be a habit. See if you can develop a journaling habit.

Your journaling should be a writing activity, not just a thinking-on-the-fly activity. The act of writing (or typing) deepens the attention you put on a particular reflection, and it allows you to more acutely observe your own thinking process. Journaling makes your learning more tangible and longer lasting. Additionally, writing can be cathartic and provide a sounding board to work out your thoughts in a much more powerful way than simply thinking about something on the go. Finally, it is also powerful to review past journal entries. We can't do that if we simply thought them but didn't write anything down.

Make It Work for You

1. **Find the mode that works for you, but make sure it involves writing versus just thinking.**

   Some people like to write in notebooks (the old-fashioned way). I have years' worth of notebooks filed away with old journals, but today, I prefer typing in my computer, smartphone notes, or online journal. My clients have the option to participate in an online journaling activity that I custom design for their program. Whatever the mode, the key to journaling is to have a platform to write regularly.

2. **Start out small.**

   If you aren't yet comfortable with the idea of journaling, start out small. Give yourself five-minute intervals (daily or at least three to four times a week) to write. Don't overburden yourself by making this into a big task.

3. **Get started by simply doing it without overthinking it or aiming for perfection.**

   Give yourself the freedom to simply write without worrying about getting it right. There's no need to have the grammar or spelling perfect. Your journal is simply a place to express authentic thoughts as they come. Go ahead and be messy!

4. **Experiment with freestyle journaling.**

   You can try out freestyle journaling and write about whatever you want. Sometimes this is just what we need. In my own online journaling program, I have a query simply called "Whassup?" I often go to this one instead of the more specific queries. One word of caution: it's okay to vent in a journal, but don't make it all about the negative. This will not serve you.

5. **Try to bring a learner's mindset to the process.**

   Speaking of venting, that's a human thing to do, but too much BMWing will fast-track you to the judger swamp. Try to keep an open mind, and remember to bring due attention to the positive with learner-oriented and appreciative inquiries (e.g., What can I do? What is going well? What do I want?).

6. **Write about a specific query or issue.**
Journaling around a question or a particular issue is also helpful. For instance, I give my clients specific journaling queries that they can reflect on regularly, such as "How did you use your strengths today?" and "How are you honouring your goal of ___?" and so on. The possibilities are endless. By focusing on a question, you are reflecting in an intentional way, and this approach can be rewarding and enlightening. It also helps ignite the writing and reflection process if you feel uncomfortable simply starting with a blank slate. See the previous tool regarding powerful questions for additional queries to journal about.

7. **Enjoy celebratory journaling.**
A wonderful habit to boost resiliency and optimism, particularly when the going is tough, is to reflect on the positive things in your life. Journaling is the ideal platform to help create this habit, and there are many ways to do this. One example is writing about what went well in your day. Doing this even when your day wasn't great is a terrific way to balance out your perspective. All too often, our focus goes towards the negative. Explicitly asking yourself to think about the positive is an emotionally intelligent behaviour that fosters resiliency, optimism, and overall well-being. I will say more on this in the chapter on honing the positivity advantage.

8. **Make it a ritual.**
While it's not imperative to journal at the same time every day, creating a ritual can help build the journaling habit if you are new to this activity. Pick a time that works for you. It can be the end of the day or the beginning. The key is to set an intention and write regularly until it becomes a habit. After time, you might find yourself craving your opportunities to sit down and write (I do!). But initially, you

might simply have to make appointments with yourself to do it. It's like going out for a bit of exercise: you might not feel like doing it at the time, but afterwards, you'll be glad you did.

9. **Review your journals.**
   Writing journals is a powerful insight generator in itself, but reading them can be just as valuable. Imagine you had a movie of your life and were able to see yourself in close-up at a particular time in your life. Well, journaling gives you that opportunity. Reading past success stories can remind you of your victories, abilities, and strengths. Reading entries about your aspirations, values, and priorities can remind you of what's important or what was important at one time. Likewise, reading about challenges and your actions might elicit awareness of some of your blind spots. Take it from me—after thirty years of journaling, I can tell you that the opportunity to read yourself is a powerful learning opportunity!

10. **Observe the difference your journaling makes.**
    I've heard clients say journaling has changed their lives. They have more optimism, resiliency, productivity, clarity, and focus, to name just a few key benefits. Take some time to observe and reflect on how you feel after you journal. The value might speak to itself.

The Pay-Off

Journaling encourages you to develop a reflective mindset, which leads to better thinking, more-positive feelings, and empowered actions—all essentials for experiencing more ease and well-being.

✓ Learn about yourself.
✓ Work out issues.
✓ Become more in charge of your thinking and your emotions.
✓ Have a valuable repository of reflections and insights that keeps on giving.

Tool #13: Clear the Cache

Now that I've had you thinking, thinking, thinking with various reflection tools, I'm going to invite you to stop thinking. Yup, it's time for a break, or as I like to say, "It's time to clear the cache." This is an expression I use in reference to clearing your mind.

In the world of computers, tech types tell us that we need to clear our computer cache now and again. If we don't do that, our computers become sluggish, process data more slowly, and just don't function optimally. They also hold on to old web pages that aren't useful anymore.

People are like that too. Today's work tends to lean fundamentally towards thinking jobs. We are at it constantly. Sometimes we can get stuck with old thinking patterns or suffer fatigue from too much thinking going on. To perform optimally, we need to deliberately take time to clear out our mental clutter to improve our thinking power, creativity, and ability for fresh ideas.

To clear our cache, we need to unplug from our current thinking activity and completely shift gears.

Have you ever noticed that some of our best ideas happen when we are not thinking—or, rather, not deliberately trying to find the answer or come up with an idea?

Experts say that sometimes the best way to solve a seemingly unsolvable problem is to simply stop trying to solve the problem and to instead walk away from it. Heed the advice from Dr. Herbert Benson, MD,[1] of Harvard Medical School and co-author with William Proctor of *The Breakout Principle*.[2] Benson and Proctor say taking breaks from thinking about an issue can trigger an inner switch that increases mental function, creativity, and productivity. Their book describes the breakout principle as a powerful mind-body impulse that severs prior mental patterns—and even in times of great stress or emotional trauma—opens an inner door to a host of personal benefits such as greater mental acuity, enhanced creativity, productivity, maximum athletic performance and spiritual performance.

Sounds amazing—I'll take two orders of that, please!

It gets better. The good news is that it is not difficult to trigger the breakout principle. According to the authors, it simply involves walking away from the activity you are focused on and shifting gears completely. You need to do something that allows your mind to remove itself from the issue you were focusing on and wander freely to any topic or thought. I've had breakout experiences driving my car, taking a shower, running, and, most recently, making potato knishes.

The Story at a Glance

In December 2012, I was all queued up during my year-end break to devote at least a few days to some of my writing projects (my book, my new website, my articles in the *Globe and Mail*,[3] etc.). When I finally had some white space to write (time with no appointments or obligations), I found myself unable to tap into my writing mode. I had another case of writer's block and couldn't get a creative thought out, never mind a sentence. I tried and tried again. Finally, I gave up (temporarily) and decided to make potato knishes that I would freeze in anticipation of my family visiting the following week.

So I got to work—potato-knish-making work, that is. Guess what happened? Sometime between sautéing the onions, rolling out the dough, and stuffing in the potato filling, I had an epiphany. Then I had another and another. I was unstoppable! Good thing I had note paper nearby so that I could jot the ideas down.

All it took to end my creative dry spell was a little break and an activity that allowed my mind to disengage from the original challenge and instead wander wherever it wanted to go. That break from intentional thinking gives the brain a chance to make connections from different parts of our brain, which generates those ahas and creative insights.

Twenty-four knishes later, I also had six shiny new ideas. At least a few of them are now in this book, on my blog, and elsewhere. And the other ideas are filed away in my "Oh bleep! Another idea!" file (see tool number seven, "Manage the Paradox of Choice at the Buffet of Life").

The Advice

Take breaks that allow you to unplug and shift gears completely. They don't have to be long breaks. Sometimes a short break will do the trick. Pick an activity that either rests your mind or engages in something that is different from the issue or activity you were trying to work on prior.

Make It Work for You

Each individual will have his or her own personal breakout triggers that work for him or her. Recognize there are different categories of potential activities to draw on. Examples include spiritual pursuits, physical activities, collaborative and altruistic pursuits, musical or cultural activities, nature, housework, repetitive actions, and, yes, knish making.

Here are some ideas to consider.

- Take a walk or take part in any other activity that allows you to step away from the issue or problem you are trying to solve.

- Engage in an activity that focuses you intently on something else. Whether it is a sport or a crossword puzzle, an activity that truly shifts your focus can help clear the cache.

- Try simple, repetitive motor activities that allow your mind to focus on something else and wander at the same time. For instance, excellent breakout of this type includes cleaning, knitting, crocheting, gardening, cooking, etc.

- Take some time for spiritual activities, such as meditation or prayer, if that's your thing.

- Include stress-reduction activities, such as spending time with someone upbeat and positive or even enjoying some time with a pet.

- Do something altruistic. Helping others gets your mind off yourself and your problems.

- Take a break even if you are not in the mood if you are feeling mentally weary. Resist the temptation to forgo your break. I've had many days when I didn't want to leave my desk to go to the gym ("Too much to do here!" I would tell myself). However, I'd go anyway and would come back fully refreshed and better able to tackle my work.

- And more! Can you come up with some activities that work for you? Create a list of potential breakout activities that would be resonant for you.

The Pay-Off

Learn to recognize when it's time to surrender, shift gears, and enjoy a renewal of energy, creativity, resourcefulness, and resilience.

- ✓ You will boost your productivity.
- ✓ You will have a chance for fresh thinking.
- ✓ A breakout activity will offer a creative boost.
- ✓ A timeout will provide a restart to your day, with more resources to tap into.

Chapter 6
Mood Matters: Hone the Positivity Advantage

What does mood have to do with taming overwhelm, handling stress, and contributing to personal and professional well-being?

Everything! Let me get straight to the point: mood matters.

A positive mood isn't just nice to have or exclusively about feeling good. Positivity and happiness are key factors that distinguish people who thrive from those who simply get by—especially during stressful times.

A positive mood has a significant impact on our brain's ability to function optimally. Mood can impact brain processes related to insight, focus, creativity, judgment, and decision making. A positive and well-managed mood is integral to taming the survival brain and can prevent those inappropriate amygdala reactions. Positive mindsets have also been shown to improve health and might even help you sleep better—another important factor in dealing with stress and overwhelm.

For some people, staying positive—even in tough times—comes naturally. Others have to learn how to do this. The good news is that we can. Positivity and happiness are skills, not a default condition.

This section provides a look at why mood matters, how and what we can control, and some practical ideas (i.e., tools) to hone the positivity advantage.

Tools → Mood Matters: Hone the Positivity Advantage

14. Check Your Positivity Ratio
15. Create a Happiness Portfolio
16. Boost the Positivity Habit with Just Minutes a Day
17. Get to Sleep

Tool #14: Check Your Positivity Ratio

Do you believe that you have the power to change your happiness potential?

Consider these three statements, and answer *true* or *false* for each of them.

1. Happiness always depends on your circumstances.
2. Happiness is a mood that you can't really change. You either feel it or you don't.
3. Some people are born happier than others.

The first two are false. The last one has some truth to it—but it's not entirely true. We have a significant amount of leverage at our disposal to boost our happiness, mood, and overall sense of positivity. In fact, we can rewire our brains with the right kind of intentional practice and habits to create more-positive mindsets. Neuroscience has taught us that, contrary to the old adage, we *can* teach an old dog new tricks—in this case, our old dog being our brains and mindset habits.

The Story at a Glance

In this section, I will do away with the usual story and will instead highlight some key research that has illuminated our understanding of happiness and positivity.

According to Sonja Lyubomirsky,[1] professor of psychology at the University of California, there are important ratios to pay attention to. Lyubomirsky is author of two books: *The How of Happiness*[2] and *The Myths of Happiness: What Should Make You Happy but Doesn't; What Shouldn't Make You Happy but Does.*[3]

Her research and that of her peers says that only 10 per cent of our sustained happiness might be determined by our circumstances, while 50 per cent of sustained happiness is determined by a set point we are born with, which explains why some people might have a more natural tendency towards happiness than others. This leaves us with 40 per cent that is completely within our power to influence. Lyubomirsky refers to this as the area for "intentional activity."

What Determines Happiness?
(Sonja Lyubomirsky, from *The How of Happiness*)

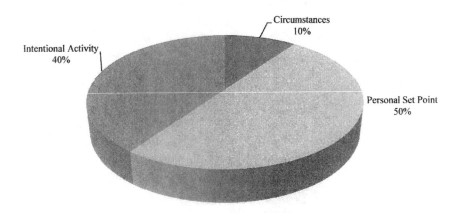

Circumstances 10%

Intentional Activity 40%

Personal Set Point 50%

The 40 Per Cent Ratio: Intentional Activity

Forty per cent is a heck of a lot—especially if you already have some equity in the heredity bank (your set point) and circumstances (when good stuff happens). It's within the intentional 40 per cent arena that we can make an enormous difference in our overall mood and happiness by intentionally engaging in activities and ways of thinking that contribute to more-positive mindsets and overall happiness. We'll get into some of these ideas in a bit, but first, here's another important ratio.

The Three-to-One Ratio

Barbara Fredrickson,[4] author of the books *Positivity*[5] and *Love 2.0*[6] and also a world-renowned expert in the field of positive psychology, outlines a compelling case for developing your positivity habit. She says we should strive for a ratio of at least three positive thoughts to one negative. Fredrickson says positivity is not an end as much as it is a means. While positivity certainly makes us feel good (an end that is worthwhile in itself!), it is also a means that broadens and expands how our minds work. A positive mindset can change how you think, which can change your entire experience of your work and life.

In earlier chapters, we explored how we can shift our mindsets by trading up bad thoughts for good ones (e.g., instead of saying, "I'll never get this pile of work done," ask, "What *can* I do?"). Fredrickson's work reinforces the benefits of this kind of thinking and says that positive thoughts can open up the doors to a more expansive, creative, and resourceful mindset.

So let's be real for a moment: bad thoughts happen. That is part of being human. So to be clear, this work isn't about removing all negative thoughts and turning into Stepford[7] happiness models. We are real people and have to deal with real stuff in our lives. According to Fredrickson, this work is about perspective shifts and changing the *frequency* of our positive thoughts towards an important tipping point that will make a significant difference in our overall well-being. Ad hoc positive thoughts aren't enough to contribute to a more positive mood if they are competing in a sea of negative thoughts and emotions.

There's some brain science behind this. It turns out our brains have a biological bias towards negativity. Perhaps for evolutionary reasons (to protect against danger), the negative thoughts stick tight, while the positive ones tend to be more slippery. Fredrickson (and many others) have shared this metaphor to illustrate the point: negative thoughts are like Velcro (sticky), and positive thoughts are like Teflon (slippery). So we have to work harder to enjoy the benefits of positive thoughts.

According to Fredrickson, the three-to-one ratio of positive to negative thoughts seems to be the tipping point that moves someone from a place of perhaps just coping, getting by, or even struggling to that which is at or closer to a state of flourishing. Her research found that when in a cluster of positive thoughts, each new positive thought has more muscle power to amplify the benefits associated with positivity.

The Advice

Make a commitment to develop your positivity habit. Create a plan much like you would for fitness, nutrition, or any other facet of well-being. Commit to observing and practising positivity. Consider both ratios introduced in this chapter. Explore ways to incorporate activities as well as mindsets that meet both the 40 per cent intentional-activity ratio and the minimum of three-to-one positive-to-negative ratio.

The remainder of this book (and many of the earlier tools) supports this notion. This tool is explicitly intended to inspire you to make the commitment to develop an awareness of your personal positivity (or otherwise) and to develop habits to further boost your positivity. There's more specific guidance on how to do so in the subsequent tools that follow.

Make It Work for You

There are hundreds of ways to develop your happiness and positivity habits. In the remaining tools in this section, we will look at some specific exercises that you can do in quick bursts of time. For now, consider these broad themes for ideas about how to get started and generate more positivity and happiness in your life.

- **Pay attention and practise noticing.**
  Awareness is a powerful place to begin. Start to pay attention and catch yourself in the moment of a negative thought and emotion, and see if you can make a switch. Often, we mindlessly go about our days and are not cognizant of how our mindset and thoughts influence our moods and actions. See earlier tools in chapter 5 ("Develop Conscious and Empowering Mindsets") for some extra help, as those tools are geared towards offering mind-shifting strategies.

- **Do an audit.**
  If you are up to it, take a particular day and do an audit of your thoughts. Find a way to quickly and easily note the frequency of your thoughts (positive versus negative). One idea is to keep a small

notebook with you to jot down observations, and at the end of the day, see how your thoughts stacked up. The purpose of this exercise is to gauge the ratio of your thoughts (even in broad strokes) and the impact on your overall mood.

- **Take the positivity-ratio online quiz.**
  Barbara Fredrickson offers a two-minute online quiz you can take on her website: www.positivityratio.com. This will give you a quick snapshot of where you stand. She also offers a program that you can download to monitor your positivity over a longer period of time.

- **Commit to creating a happiness plan.**
  This can be an evolving plan (as part of your overall well-being plan) that starts with one or just a few commitments. For instance, you might decide to engage in more-fulfilling activities to feed your 40 per cent ratio of intentional happiness-generating activity. Or you might try to monitor your thoughts more diligently and practise new ways of thinking, as per earlier tools. There are hundreds of possibilities, but the key is to intentionally create a plan that you commit to, track, and monitor. There are many areas to choose from to create more happiness, and a diversified approach can work better than an approach that focuses on only one tactic. The next tool will provide some guidance on how to create your personal happiness portfolio.

The Pay-Off

Developing a positive mindset is a critical factor for boosting your capacity to thrive—even in times of "crazy busy."

✓ You will experience more joy, happiness, and personal mojo in the moments of life.
✓ You will become more optimistic, even when the going is tough.
✓ You will think better and open up your mind with more creativity and resourcefulness to handle the tough loads.
✓ You will be healthier.
✓ And so much more!

Tool #15: Create a Happiness Portfolio

The previous tool encouraged you to commit to a positive mindset. We looked at some powerful research that illuminated how much we can control and what kind of ratios to aim for to get the happiness and positive advantage. In this tool, we will look at some themes for creating a happiness portfolio for your life.

Why a portfolio? Much like financial experts encourage you to diversify your financial portfolio for an appropriate balance for your financial life, experts specializing in positive psychology also advocate a diversified-portfolio approach for happiness and well-being.

In July 2012, a gathering of experts at the Canadian Positive Psychology Conference[1] featured several speakers who highlighted this notion and spoke about distinct areas that can be part of a happiness portfolio—each meeting different needs. They spoke of hedonistic pursuits (focusing on pleasure) and eudaemonic activities (focusing on meaning, self-realization, and personal growth). However, there's also a third dimension that often gets left out: focusing on complete relaxation, or doing nothing and just being. We need all three.

A truly balanced happiness portfolio will do more for your overall well-being than drawing only from one dimension. The specific pursuits and the time spent will vary for each individual, but the key is to pay attention and create the mix that works for you.

The Story at a Glance

A client I'll call Carynne came to a coaching session a little low in spirits and shared with me she had been feeling a bit flat. She couldn't find her spark and motivation.

I knew she had been going through a stressful period at work. Putting in long hours was the norm for her. But when we explored further, it appeared that she was not only working extra hard during this demanding period but also dealing with a workload that had become pretty humdrum, or uninspiring and somewhat boring. Her files were made up of routine work and not stretching her development in any way or feeding her core values around learning and personal growth. As she worked harder than ever with an abundance of billable hours, the rewards aside from her financial gain were slim to none. At the same time, the stuff of life away from work had also become routine and a bit stale—errands, routines, and blah, blah, blah. She needed some mojo (energy, spark, inspiration)!

So we brainstormed together and, from our discussion, came up with a few ideas. In broad strokes, she discovered that she needed to find new clients who would interest and challenge her and ultimately add more meaning to her work. Outside of work, she decided to get involved in activities that engaged her passion and strength for creativity, specifically her love of writing and storytelling. And finally, she wanted a little bit of time to just relax, hang out, and breathe. In just one hour, she had the beginnings of a portfolio plan that would meet different needs. Her next step was to explore and try to fill in those parts with specific activities (or non-activities, in the case of her relax-and-hang-out goal). Putting that intention in place with a specific framework for her plan woke her up, and she immediately began to feel more energized and alive.

The Advice

Step back from your work and life regularly to evaluate if your life portfolio is sufficiently meeting your happiness and fulfilment needs. Are the activities in your work and life providing the right balance between pleasurable pursuits, growth activities, and rest and renewal? Are you doing enough that energizes and fuels your mind, spirit, and body? Is your portfolio leaving you flat or, worse, depleting you? Assess your current reality, and then, if needed, tweak, diversify, explore, and experiment to create a more balanced and fulfilling happiness portfolio.

Make It Work for You

There are hundreds of ways to develop your happiness portfolio. Within the past decade, the field of positive psychology has exploded with research and new insights on what essential ingredients help contribute to happiness, fulfilment, and our overall well-being. Here are some themes to consider.

- **Develop (and refresh) meaningful goals.**
  Martin Seligman,[2] the founder of the positive psychology movement and author of *Authentic Happiness*[3] as well as *Flourishing*,[4] says the conditions for flourishing come from five pillars,[5] two of which include accomplishments and meaning and purpose in our lives. Our moods can wilt when we are without new goals or not connected to a sense of purpose. Often, in the busyness of life, we forget to refresh and add new goals.

  When feeling flat, ask yourself what goals are inspiring you and if it is time to create new ones. They need not always be big goals. Smaller ones work too.

- **Use more of your strengths in daily life.**
  A key strategy for fulfilment is to use more of your natural strengths, particularly those that are associated with your values and core character virtues. Many of us operate in our lives blind to these core strengths, but the more we use them in our daily lives, the more we will feel fulfilled and experience success. You can discover your character and signature strengths with an assessment at www.VIAcharacter. org.[6] You will see that depending on your strengths, the potential activities will reveal themselves. For instance, if curiosity and love of learning are signature strengths of yours, then engaging in learning opportunities that you are curious about will boost your fulfilment.

  Learn what your signature strengths are, and then find novel ways to use them in your work and life.

- **Seek positive social connections.**
  Another pillar for flourishing and positivity is good relationships and social interaction. The late Christopher Peterson,[7] also a monumental contributor and early founder of the positive psychology movement, coined the expression "People matter" in reference to this particular pillar. Peterson, author of *Positive Psychology Primer*[8] and *Pursuing the Good Life*,[9] was noted for his work on optimism, health, character, and well-being. He frequently referred to an array of research affirming the connection between the quality of our social interaction and relationships and our well-being.

  Make sure your life has enough "people connection" in it. Explore new avenues for social and relationship opportunities, including, family, friends, work, neighbourhood, community, etc.

- **Experience awe and wonder.**
  In our busy lives of rush, rush, rush, we rarely take time to pause and smell the roses. Taking some time to experience even small bursts of awe and wonder in your life can inspire a more positive mood—even beyond the moment. If you love nature, get out more; if beauty is your thing, go see an exhibit. If you love artful dance—well, you get the point—cha-cha-cha!

  Identify your sources of awe, and go out and get more of them!

- **Go for a run or walk or swim.**
  We can't separate our physical well-being from our emotional well-being. Part of your happiness plan should include attention to your physical well-being. In fact, one of the best mood boosters is aerobic activity, which releases endorphins in the body.

  Go for a brisk walk or run (or engage in some other aerobic activity) and get a nice dose of endorphins and the added benefit of having time to clear the cache (see tool number thirteen).

- **Have fun.**
  Oh yes, let's not forget those pursuits that are simply for pleasure. Life can get pretty earnest at times. A balanced happiness plan will also have ample pleasurable pursuits. While any of the above categories might bring pleasure, some activities and hobbies can simply be for fun. Indulge in a movie marathon, cook up something special, see a comedy show, or do whatever else you find fun—just do it. The halo effect of a good time can spill over to work and give you some extra energy to tackle the loads.

  Make sure you know what you love to do for fun, and include some of these activities in your happiness plan.

- **Stop and do nothing.**
  Do you leave any white space in your life to simply do nothing? If large chunks of free time aren't possible for you, how about stolen moments here and there to sit, think, meditate, or simply just be?

  Learn to press the pause button.

- **Monitor, reflect, revise, and then rinse and repeat.**
  The ideas above are directional only and represent just a few drops in a sea of potential ideas to contribute to your happiness portfolio. Make it your own by experimenting, tinkering, observing, and doing again and again. It's not a one-time deal. It's a habit to nurture throughout life.

The Pay-Off

Developing a portfolio approach to happiness can bring many levels of fulfilment to your life.

- ✓ You will experience more meaning and a sense of purpose.
- ✓ You will feel more vibrant by participating in energy-infusing activities.
- ✓ You will recognize that even when life is "crazy busy," balance is possible.
- ✓ You will fortify your ability to handle the tough times.

Tool #16: Develop the Positivity Habit with Just Minutes a Day

When work and life go into overdrive, our most precious resource—time—becomes even more strained and sparse. But practising positivity doesn't have to consume a lot of time. There are powerful practices that take only minutes yet can significantly boost your positivity and mood—if you practise them daily.

The Story at a Glance

In 2011, a company called me to see if I could help out with one of their leaders. The manager, whom we will call Bryce, was struggling with a significantly increased workload and some additional pressure at home. His energy and mood were in serious decline, his health was suffering, and his performance was starting to teeter and head south. The company felt he was a keeper, but clearly he was having trouble and was at risk of losing his performance edge and well-being. So we started to do some work together and, over time, incorporated many of the exercises I've introduced throughout this book. Learning new skills and developing new habits can take time, but we also wanted him to experience some relief in short order and get some positivity momentum going right away, so I introduced a few exercises he could do regularly (daily if possible) that were not time intensive.

The exercises specifically focused on getting him to shift his perspective to an authentic and positive mindset. He took a few moments to journal each day, reflecting on the positive details of the day and all he had accomplished despite the never-ending to-do lists (see below for further details on the "Three Good Things Today" and "Ta-Da" exercises—two examples of the kinds of journaling reflections he engaged in).

His time investment was only a few minutes a day, but the pay-off was extraordinary. Within only one week, he reported a significant shift. He was motivated and able to tackle his loads with more focus and resilience.

He kept this habit going, along with other practices we focused on in our work together. At the end of the year, Bryce felt his new habits helped him stay resilient, focused, and optimistic even as his workloads got tougher. His bosses noticed too!

Don't take my word for it; countless others have demonstrated similar results. In the January 2012 issue of *Harvard Business Review*,[1] Shawn Achor of Good Think Inc. wrote about similar work with various organizations. In particular, he shared some research he conducted with tax managers at KPMG in New York and New Jersey in December 2008. This was just before the worst tax season in decades. Achor set out to prove that by engaging in one brief positive exercise every day for as little as a few weeks, you can have some lasting benefits. He invited the managers to choose one of five activities that involved only short investments of time yet were intended to boost their positive mindsets.

The activities (some are similar to those I work with) included jotting down three good things they were grateful for; writing a positive message to someone in their social network; meditating at their desk for two minutes; exercising for ten minutes; and taking two minutes to journal on the most meaningful thing they had experienced in the last twenty-four hours.

Did the experiment work? Yes, it did! After three weeks, the managers who participated in the exercises scored significantly higher in a range of metrics measuring their sense of well-being, life satisfaction, and happiness compared with the control group who did not engage in the activities. Four months later, the participants still showed a substantial advantage over the control group. Keep in mind what happened during those four months: the worst economic crisis in decades. The pressure was immense.

The lesson learned is that developing a positivity habit doesn't have to be time consuming. And as I said earlier, the brain has a lot more neuroplasticity than was initially understood. By practising new ways of thinking and creating new positive thinking habits, we can create new neuropaths in the brain, leading to more-sustained positive attitudes, increased resilience, more-optimistic mindsets, and even health advantages.

The Advice

Commit to developing a positivity habit with short practices[2] you can incorporate daily. Try them out. Notice the difference. Rinse and repeat.

Make It Work for You

Choose from the following exercises,[3] commit to at least one of these activities daily for a few weeks, and see what happens. Ideally, commit to doing them every day for life! Shake them up and rotate them if you choose. By doing different exercises, you can keep them fresh (the brain loves novelty). Or choose the one that is most resonant for you on any given day.

- **Gratitude at work.**
  Take a few moments to write down what you are most grateful for in your work and life at any given time. Even when times are challenging, there are good things we must pay attention to.

  Another positivity boost comes through expressing gratitude to others. Take a few moments to explicitly thank someone for something you appreciate. You can do this verbally or write a note. Through this exercise, you will not only make the recipient of your gratitude feel good but also get the rewards of giving gratitude as well. Another way to do this is to pick a buddy to exchange your gratitude lists with in a conversation.

- **Three good things that happened today—and why.**
  I love this exercise! Take a few moments at the end of each day and write out three good things that happened that day. Granted, there are days when a lot seems to be going wrong. And as our brain bias defaults to the negative, it is easy to dwell on what went wrong. This

exercise invites us to intentionally balance our perspective and appreciate the stuff that is going well. The list can mark small wins or big wins; it doesn't matter.

In addition to writing out the three good things, it's also helpful to reflect on the reasons they went well or why you consider them to be good. For instance, if you wrote, "The meeting went well," then the *why* might be related to how you prepared, your ability to think on your feet, or your knowledge—or something else. By acknowledging your role in something that went well, you build efficacy and confidence, which can also be big mood boosters.

- **What went well?**
  This is a different version of listing three good things. Often, we rush by our successes and don't take time to acknowledge them. We are off to the next task. Writing out what went well gives us a celebratory moment and a sense of satisfaction.

  It can be a small victory, but as long as it's meaningful, it has merit. Giving attention to what went well is especially important during tough, stressful situations that might not have gone as well as you would have liked overall. For instance, this exercise is helpful when evaluating a particular project or event and balancing out the feedback to yourself. If you felt the task didn't go as well as you had hoped, then explicitly focusing on this part of the evaluation balances the perspective.

  If you are a leader of a group, this is also a great exercise to do verbally with your team. Build on success. This doesn't mean you ignore the other parts (i.e., what can be improved), but often, what went well gets short-changed. Boosting team morale isn't always as heavy a lift as one thinks. Acknowledging the big and small wins regularly can make a significant difference to individual and team morale.

- **From "to-do" to "ta-da!"**

   If you like to cross off tasks on a list, you'll love this exercise. This is more than crossing off your to-dos. This activity asks you to take a blank page and write out highlights of what *did* get done. It is the antidote to that feeling of the never-ending list. Remember the Zeigarten effect discussed with tool number one? Our minds more easily remember unfinished tasks than those we complete. This exercise invites you to celebrate what is getting done. It's a wonderful way to complete your day and will give you more peace of mind. And I bet more often than not, you will be surprised how much you accomplished.

- **Meditation—even for nonmeditators.**

   Perhaps meditation can be considered a power tool in your repertoire of mindful tools. Much like many of the tools shared in this book, meditation helps you focus inwards, become more mindful, and reap the rewards of greater peace, ease, focus, and confidence. Keep in mind that the earlier tools introduced, such as journaling, asking powerful questions, etc., are also oriented towards being more mindful.

   If you've never meditated before, rest assured that you don't have to spend hours to benefit from the rewards. Even short bursts of meditating can make a difference. Stilling your mind for a few minutes regularly can create positive changes in your brain, body, and spirit, leading to a healthier, happier, and more productive you.

   If you've never done it before, set small goals—perhaps meditating for just a few moments at a time. Consider joining a group or taking a class. Or you might want to download or buy some guided meditation CDs—whatever works for you. The key is to try it out and see what happens.

- **Run, walk, or cha-cha-cha!**
  Okay, this one might take a bit more than just a few minutes. But it doesn't necessarily have to take a lot of time. Even smaller doses of exercise can make a difference (fifteen to thirty minutes a day).

As I mentioned earlier (per tool number fifteen), aerobic exercise that gets your muscles moving, your heart pumping, and your blood flowing isn't just healthy for your body; it's one of the best positivity boosters around. Aerobic activity releases those yummy endorphins that feel oh-so good! Regular aerobic activity is also a key contributor to neuroplasticity. Yup, by moving our bodies, we help build our brain's capacity to develop those new positive neuroconnections.

If you can't get to the gym or find the time to exercise after work, consider building exercise time into your day. For instance, if you take public transit to work, then get off a few stops earlier and give yourself a minimum of a twenty-minute walk. Or take the stairs instead of using the elevator. Be creative and find bits of time throughout the day. It does add up. Most importantly, when time-crunched, remember to ask yourself what *can you* do (per tool number ten)!

The Pay-Off

Small investments of time in positivity exercises pay off in big dividends that sustain your well-being.

- ✓ You will have a fortified mood that lasts well beyond the time you invest.
- ✓ You will increase your resilience and optimism.
- ✓ You will experience sharper, clearer thinking and more creativity.
- ✓ You will have a healthier mind, body, and spirit and a much more productive you!

Tool #17: Get to Sleep

Do you remember never wanting to go to sleep or take a nap as a child? A reminder that youth is wasted on the young! Now, as adults, it seems we can't get enough sleep—or, rather, many of us aren't getting enough quality sleep.

Lack of quality sleep is becoming an issue for too many people. For some, it happens by choice. We are a society addicted to productivity. As we try to squeeze more out of our days, sometimes we do so at the expense of sleep—staying up late or waking up an extra hour earlier to squeeze in a workout or get a jump on the workday or simply handle the commute to work.

For others, lack of sleep is not by choice. I hear many people complain that they can't fall asleep, can't stay asleep, or wake up too soon—sometimes in the middle of the night.

It's time to wake up to the issue of not enough sleep!

Getting ample quality sleep is imperative for optimal performance, resilience, and well-being. Sleep provides critical recovery and restoration for multiple biological systems in our body from the wear and tear of our waking hours. As important as this is for our body, sleep is even more critical for the brain's functions, such as memory, creative processing, and emotional regulation. Remember the concept of leadership lockdown syndrome introduced in chapter 2? Poor sleep with a bad mood and too much stress can greatly compromise our critical-thinking skills. In fact, poor sleep can negatively impact our mood. No wonder sleep is so important!

How much sleep do we need? Individuals' needs vary, but experts say that on average, adults need about seven to nine hours daily.

The Advice

Get to bed! Go to sleep! Get your ample Zs. And if you are having a tough time falling or staying asleep, make a commitment to learn the source of your sleep challenges and try out new strategies to help you combat the issue. Create a sleep plan as part of your overall well-being plan.

I'll do away with the "Story at a Glance" section so that I can get straight to the goods (although if you have a good bedtime story, I invite you to read it!).

Make It Work for You

Here are some tips and ideas to put you to sleep (literally, not metaphorically, I hope!).

- **Set the intention to get enough sleep.**
  Go to bed at a deliberate time to get enough hours. Sometimes people get busy and distracted and don't realize the time. This is especially true for night owls ("Oh, I didn't realize it's already one o'clock in the morning!"). Make it a point to go to bed by a certain hour so that you can get your seven to nine hours of sleep and get your body used to a routine. If you are lucky enough to not have other sleep issues, your solution might be as simple as setting an intention and following through.

- **Create a ritual of habits that will optimize your ability to sleep.**
  If you've been working, frazzled, and rushing throughout your day, then make a habit to wind down, disengage, and calm your mind at least an hour before you get into bed. If you go to bed frazzled, you might find it difficult to fall asleep or stay asleep. Try out some of the positivity or journaling exercises introduced in earlier chapters to help you calm your mind, complete your day, and shift your thoughts away from work or other pressing issues.

- **Enjoy some milk and cookies before bed.**

  Ahh, now we're talking! Yes, you read this right. I got this tip from Aileen Burford-Mason, PhD,[1] a cell biologist, scientist, and nutritional expert who wrote the book *Eat Well, Age Better.*[2] The point of the milk-and-cookies idea is to get some tryptophan into our brain to kick up the release of serotonin, which can help us sleep. Milk (and other proteins) is a great source of tryptophan, but alone, it can't cut across the blood–brain barrier. It needs a bit of help. The insulin from the carbohydrates and sugar in the cookies helps break that blood barrier and—ahhh—produces a nice sleepy feeling. Burford-Mason provides a more credible, scientific explanation, but I needed little to convince me to have milk and cookies before bed. By the way, I've tried replacing the milk and cookies with the occasional ice-cream treat (which worked for me!) or less-sugary fare, such as whole-wheat toast. Remember, the tip is a small snack, such as a glass of milk and a cookie, not the whole row of cookies or a heavy meal!

- **Create darkness in your room.**

  Darkness helps create melatonin—another essential ingredient needed for good sleep. Apparently, even slight rays of light creeping in can interrupt the production of melatonin and disrupt sleep. Aileen Burford-Mason suggests using an eye mask to create more darkness. I tried it. I'm sure I look funny, but it works! You might also consider limiting your use of electrical devices, such as computers, smartphones, and electronic reading devices, just before bed.

- **Go easy on the caffeine and red wine.**

  While I found I have to stop consuming caffeine by early afternoon in order to sleep well, you might have your own caffeine time boundary. The key is to pay attention to this issue, as caffeine can impede your sleeping cycle. Also, watch out for the effects of wine and other alcoholic beverages. Drinking some might make you initially sleepy, but alcohol can act as a stimulant and can keep you up later.

- **Be aware of any nutritional deficiencies.**
  Your medications might be keeping you awake. If you are on medications or not eating right, there are repercussions from a bionutritional perspective that will impact your sleep. In her book, Burford-Mason discusses magnesium and the importance it plays in our ability to sleep and manage stress. Many prescription drugs deplete our magnesium levels. Apparently, high-blood-pressure drugs are one of the worst culprits. It's worth checking out this issue and seeing someone who specializes in holistic nutrition, especially if you are on medications for other health issues. The medical field at large does not typically bring nutritional considerations to their prescription approaches. There are easy things you can do to balance out the deficiencies, but you need to be aware of what they are and might need some professional guidance to customize a plan for your particular needs.

- **Don't bring stress to bed.**
  Yup, stress will rob you of a good night's sleep if you let it. There are many ways to alleviate or at least park the stress that can keep us awake at night. Many of the earlier chapters address this. Read, rinse, and repeat.

- **Exercise.**
  According to the results of the National Sleep Foundation's 2013 Sleep in America poll,[3] people who exercise are significantly more likely to experience quality sleep. While those who exercise vigorously are most likely to report quality sleep, a non-exerciser can improve his or her sleep vastly simply by starting to do some exercise, even at a moderate level. Walking for fifteen to twenty minutes a day might make a difference if you typically don't walk at all. Start with what you *can* do (see tool number ten), and build up from there.

The Pay-Off

Creating the right habits can help you get quality sleep.

- ✓ You will have a sharper brain and improve your thinking ability.
- ✓ You will tap into a more resourceful, resilient you.
- ✓ You will cope better when life throws you curves and bigger loads.
- ✓ You will maximize your potential to build new positive neuropaths (and brain habits).

Part III: What's Next?

Chapter 7

Parts Not Assembled:
Build Your Well-Being Plan

If you have read this far, I hope you have taken away ideas that will contribute to your own well-being plan to bring more ease into your life. If you have read just a few sections that piqued your interest, that's okay too!

This last section is about applying the ideas that resonate with you. First, let's revisit what this book set out to do.

I recognize that these are times of unprecedented busyness, and the purpose of *Ease* wasn't about making your life easy per se. Rather, the purpose was to help you minimize the burden and stress associated with increasingly heavy loads in work and life and develop habits that maximize your personal and professional well-being.

Remember, the definition of *ease* is "to free from something that pains, disquiets, or burdens; to take away or lessen, alleviate; to give freedom or relief (as from pain or discomfort)."

This book provided seventeen tools and loads of ideas to help you do just that. It's not a complete list. You have your own strategies, ideas, and versions of many of the tips presented. The possibilities are endless.

What to do with all these ideas?

While this book provides tools to help you cope and flourish during times of unprecedented busy, no part (or parts) in isolation will do the whole trick. Pick your spots, try them out, fine-tune them, and take action. Commit to a lifelong, evolving personal and professional well-being plan.

See the "Exercises" section for guidance and reminders to help you get started on any of the areas that resonate with you.

Guidance and Tips to Help You Build Your Plan

Here are some helpful tips and reminders as you build your plan.

- **Keep in mind that no one tool will always work for any given situation.**
  Some of the ideas might work for a while, but to keep them fresh, you might need to shake them up or try something else. For instance, the "Three Good Things" exercise often does the trick for me when I need to balance my perspective and give due attention to the positive. But sometimes I need to look for another tool for a particular day or situation. I'll go out for a run; clear the cache; get a good night's sleep; or ask a bunch of new learner questions to shift my mind—or something else. The point is to not look at any one particular tool as the panacea or magic wand but, rather, to be in a dynamic process and look at the variety of tools and strategies at your disposal.

- **Try different tools to keep things fresh.**
  Creating new habits and neuropaths in the brain requires practice and repetition, but it also requires novelty. Sometimes I will go for a long stretch using a particular strategy, but shaking things up helps challenge our perspective and open our minds to different views. Novelty is also a contributor to maximizing neuroplasticity, helping our brains create new connections. So balance the frequent and regular use of the tools that work with some freshening-up strategies.

- **Make it your own.**
  If you liked an idea in this book but you have a better way of expressing it or applying it, then please do that. The tools are there for you as guidance—to use as you see fit. Make them your own!

- **Right-size your plan.**
  For some people, starting with just a few small changes is the way to go and can make a profound difference. Others like to play it big

and might dive into many of the themes and tools presented at once. Whatever your preference, make sure you right-size the plan for you.

- **Evolve your plan.**
  Your well-being plan needs to adjust as you and your life evolve. When I proclaimed I was starting a well-being plan in early 2012, it certainly wasn't my first foray into well-being. I've been at it my entire life (focusing on fitness, nutrition, and emotional well-being). But in creating a new plan, I put a focus on specific dimensions that needed my attention at that time in my life. This is what I'm encouraging you to do. Evolve your plan as you live and progress; test things out. Add things, modify things, try out new ideas, build on existing ideas— keep your plan alive.

- **Have fun.**
  Oh yes, this book isn't meant to add more work to your life! Try to have a bit of fun with this. As I reinforced in chapter 6, fun and pleasure need to be part of the overall strategy.

Exercises

Here are some exercises to help you apply some of the book's ideas and tools in your work and life.

Pick Your Spots—Priority Areas of Focus

Identify the areas that you feel are your highest priorities right now. Perhaps it's getting better organized or learning to become more mindful and develop more-empowering mindsets with regard to a particular situation. Or that mood and mojo thing—do you need to inject more positivity into your life? How about sleep—can you improve on your Zs? Start with the most important priorities for you right now.

The most important areas I want to focus on now are the following:

_____

_____

_____

Organize the Mind and Avoid the Mind-Full Syndrome

Here are three things I will focus on to help me manage all the stuff I have to do in a way that works with the brain, not against it (choose from your toolkit):

1. _____

2. _____

3. _____

To get a grip on my schedule, here are some changes I can make:

1. _____

2. _____

3. _____

To reduce my frazzle and overzealous multitasking habit, I will commit myself to some focus time.

I will schedule (amount of time) _____ per (week or day) _____ to focus on (project/activity) _____.

I will also look outside of my workdays for focus time. Here's how:

_____

Learn to say no.
1. The people I have trouble saying no to are _____
2. The situations I have trouble saying no to are _____
3. My limiting beliefs around saying no are _____
4. More-empowering beliefs are _____
5. In the next week, I will practise saying no to _____
6. In my own buffet of life, here's where I can trim or say no so that I don't suffer from overindulging: _____

Develop Conscious (Mindful) and Empowering Mindsets

Meet Your Inner Critics
I've met one of my critics! His/her name is _____
He/she looks like _____
He/she shows up when (trigger) _____
When I notice my critic, I can choose other perspectives and voices to listen to. For example, a more reasonable perspective is _____

_____

Climb Your Mountains with Ease
These are my current mountains (projects, tasks): _____
I can chunk them down by starting with _____

Develop a Bank of Powerful Questions
There were a lot of questions introduced in this book. Start to create a bank of questions by listing the ones that were most resonant for you. Visit your bank regularly to remind yourself of these simple yet powerful

questions to help you deal with situations. Feel free to attribute them to a particular purpose (e.g., "When I'm feeling stuck, I will ask myself this question"). You might want to keep some of your favourite ones extra visible—for example, on a poster or note where you can see it regularly.

My Starting Bank of Questions includes:

_____

_____

_____

Journal

Start to develop your journaling habit by committing to small chunks of time and doing it regularly. Pick a time, and create a ritual. Once the habit sticks, you can shake it up.

I will journal at this time _____ on (list days) _____.

Hint: You might also want to list some questions or topics that you will draw on for your journaling (e.g., three good things) or draw from the exercises outlined in the tool.

Clear the Cache

These are the kinds of activities I like to do to clear the cache:

List activities that you can do when you only have short amounts of time (e.g., fifteen to twenty minutes):

List the activities you can do with longer stretches of time (e.g., an hour or more):

Mind Your Mood and Hone the Positivity Habit

My positivity ratio on (date) _____ was _____.
(Go to www.positivityratio.com to take the online positivity-ratio quiz.)

119

Boost your positivity by using more of your character and signature strengths. Go to www.VIAcharacter.org and complete the VIA strengths survey. List your top (five or so) signature strengths below.

1. _____
2. _____
3. _____
4. _____
5. _____

I will intentionally use more of my strength(s), including _____, in the following ways:

1. _____
2. _____
3. _____

Here are some other ways that I will boost my positivity habit in my daily life. (Choose from the areas outlined in the chapter or come up with your own.)

People (Relationships and Social Connections): I will focus on developing the following relationships and social opportunities: _____

_____

Awe and Wonder: I will engage in more of the following (e.g., nature, museums, other): _____

Gratitude: I will practise gratitude daily by _____

Pursuit of Meaningful Goals: I will pursue the following goal: _____

_____

Pleasure and Fun: I will do more of _____

Exercise: I will incorporate the following exercise into my week (list exercise, duration, and frequency): _____

Doing Nothing: I will make some time to press the pause button and just relax. I will try to make time for this at least _____ times a week and _____ minutes a day.

Three-Minute Exercises:

Choose from the positivity journaling activities below and/or add your own. Practise daily to create a habit, but remember to occasionally shake them up. See chapter 6 (tool number sixteen) for more information.

1. Here's What I Am Grateful for Today
2. Three Good Things That Happened Today
3. What Went Well
4. Ta-Da!

Sleep Plan:

Here's what I will do to ensure I get more quality sleep and strive for seven to nine hours per night (see chapter 6, tool number seventeen).

_____

My Happiness Portfolio:

I will add the following activities to round out my happiness portfolio:

_____

_____

_____

Want More? Engage for a Deeper Dive

If you would like to explore any of these ideas, tools, and strategies further, I invite you to get in touch for a deeper dive. I'll be offering additional resources, programs, and opportunities to engage with me and a community of others who, like yourself, want to experience more ease and well-being in these times of "crazy busy."

Here's how to stay in touch and experience more *Ease* in your work and personal life:

- Visit the websites www.EaseRX.com and www.bigcheesecoaching.com.

- Join our community by signing up for the newsletter.

- Consider inviting me to speak to your people (at work, a conference, or other).

- Invite me to speak to your bookclub via Skype

- Got another idea? Bring it on, and get in touch directly by sending an email to eileen@EaseRX.com to learn more about programs and opportunities that might be a fit for you, your team, or your organization.

Here's to you! May you experience great success with an abundance of ease and well-being in your personal and professional life!

Acknowledgments

As I reflect on the list of people I want to thank, it is worth noting that gratitude consistently shows up as my number-one character strength on the VIA strengths survey. No surprise—I feel so much gratefulness in my life and particularly in the gifts along the way that helped me write my first book. This is a big accomplishment on my personal bucket list, and I couldn't have gotten here without all the influences and support in my professional and personal life.

As I think about who these people are, I can't help but cast a significantly wider net beyond just those who have helped with the actual task of book writing. There are so many people who have helped support, shape, and grow me in my own path of learning and living, personally and professionally. This book really is an expression of a long-held passion that I've been nurturing this past decade: to inspire positivity and well-being in the lives of others.

Some of these people are close to me, and others I know only professionally. There are also some whom I haven't met personally but who have had a profound impact on me. "Thank you, everyone" just isn't going to cut it, but it needs to be said, because although I highlight some special people in the following notes, there are many others who also deserve to be recognized. For those not listed formally in these pages, please know you are noted indelibly in my heart, and I appreciate you all so much.

So here goes.

Thank you to my clients, past and present, who teach me so much as we learn and grow together and who inspired the many stories and anecdotes shared in these pages.

Thanks to Janice Turner at CPA (formerly CICA), who has invited me to be an annual presenter on the roster of their webinar series. Notably, I appreciated the opportunity I had to present my "Bogged Down and Overwhelmed—Tips to Handle It" webinar, which formed the basis for much of this book. More than 3,500 people registered for this event, and the positive feedback was part of the impetus for writing this book.

Thank you to the team at the *Globe and Mail*, who have welcomed me as a regular contributor to *Globe Careers*. A particularly big thank-you goes to Gillian Livingston, the current *Globe Careers* editor, who is so supportive and always a pleasure to work with. I also want to thank others at the *Globe Careers* team whom I have worked with over the years, including Dianne Nice, Ian Morfitt, Terry Brodie, Wallace Immen, Barbara Smith, and many others. My experience writing with the *Globe* has been wonderful and in part has provided me with the courage to write my first book.

To Elizabeth Hoyle, who started as my boss in my first "real" job in Toronto and became a mentor and then a friend and, at times, a mentee (we take turns mentoring each other!), thank you for your friendship and generosity throughout the years. In particular, thank you for your supreme generosity in bringing members from your team at H2 Central, Marketing & Communications in to help me with my book cover (kudos and thanks to Liam Hoyle, Don Hall, and Samantha Hill).

Once upon a time, people in serious business environments did not talk about things like positivity, happiness, mindfulness, and thriving—or if they did, it was considered a bit too woo-woo to be taken seriously. That has changed, and I am eternally grateful to the army of scientists, academics, and brilliant folks from the worlds of positive psychology, neuroscience, and leadership who have brought tremendous credibility to the science of well-being. Notable gratitude goes to Martin Seligman, the father of positive psychology, for starting it all (the science of well-being) and to the late Christopher Peterson, who was a giant of a contributor to this field. Chris sadly passed away in October 2012, but he left a legacy of profound inspiration and wisdom in this evolving field. I had the privilege of taking a master class on well-being led by Chris Peterson in 2011 and appreciate what a blessing it was that I had this opportunity to learn from him.

More recently, I have had the opportunity to join a special Master class with Mentor Coach lead by the exceptional Barbara Fredrickson, the foremost expert on the science of positive emotions. Her work (along with her team) has made a profound contribution to the understanding of the connection between positive emotions and well-being. I am in awe of her work and grateful for this powerful learning opportunity.

A big thank-you to Ben Dean of Mentor Coach for bringing many of the world's most renowned experts in well-being and positive psychology to the learning community. Ben makes these people (such as the above-mentioned luminaries) and their wealth of knowledge accessible to professionals such as myself, and I'm grateful for the abundance of opportunities to learn and connect with a passionate community of people interested in the vast topic of well-being.

There are so many teachers who have taught me and inspired me along the way that I could not possibly mention them all. Still, special mention must go to my earliest teachers at Adler International, including Dorothy Greenaway, Melissa Sinclair, Darlene Chrissley, and Adria Trowhill, who got me started on this journey of coaching and were foundational to my lifelong passion for this and related fields. As well, Linda Page, the fearless leader as president at Adler International, deserves acknowledgment for her stance on the importance of research in the emerging coaching (and related) fields—as well, for her passion and insights connecting neuroscience to the power of coaching.

I also thank Kim George, founder of the Abundance Intelligence Institute*, who was an "abundant" contributor in my learning journey. I am also enormously grateful to Ann Betz and Ursual Pottinga, co-founders of BEabove Leadership, for their superb advanced coach training on neuroscience, consciousness, and transformation. I am blessed and better for having had the opportunity to participate in their program.

Being part of a book club has kept me connected to my love of reading and invited me to step outside of my usual work-related reading. I thank all my peeps at the Monday Night Book Club for six years and counting and for all the lively discussions, book reviews, encounters with authors, and way too much eating at our monthly meetings. I look forward to being invited as the speaker when we review my book!

Thanks to all of the friends, family, and myriad of other supporters who encouraged me and rallied great enthusiasm for my book project each step of the way.

I'd like to give a particular shout-out to Terry Fallis, who wears many hats as an award-winning Canadian author (many times over, including the prestigious Stephen Leacock and CBC Canada Reads awards) and as a co-founder of a very successful full-service communications consulting agency. Terry is a superstar in both worlds, and despite knowing first-hand what "crazy busy" is all about, he took time to generously offer me guidance, advice, and support for *Ease* as well as a wonderful endorsement. Thanks, Ter!

Notably, the biggest thanks go to Mom and Dad (Sylvia and Sam Chadnick), my most ardent supporters, for their wisdom in knowing when it was time to encourage me to keep going when I was feeling tired and stuck and when it was time to remind me to heed my own advice to stop and clear the cache.

And to my readers, thank you for taking a chance and investing your time to read this book. Welcome to ease.

With gratitude,
Eileen

Notes

Chapter 1: Introduction

1. *Merriam-Webster OnLine*, s.v. "ease," accessed August 11, 2013, http://www.merriam-webster.com/dictionary/ease.
2. *Merriam-Webster OnLine*, s.v. "well-being," accessed August 11, 2013, http://www.merriam-webster.com/dictionary/wellbeing.

Chapter 2: Deconstructing Overwhelm

1. Dr. David Rock coined the term *neuroleadership* in 2006. He heads up the NeuroLeadership Group. See www.neuroleadership.com for more information.
2. The term *leadership lockdown syndrome* was coined by neuroscientists Jessica Payne and Stephen Thomas for a presentation made at the NeuroLeadership conference in 2011. See http://blog.davidrock.net/2011/12/2011-neuroleadership-summit-day-3.html for a story posted by Dr. David Rock.
3. NeuroLeadership conference (2011), http://neuroleadership.org/summits/2011Summit.shtml.

Chapter 4/Tool #1: Write It Down

1. *Merriam-Webster OnLine*, s.v. "Zeigarnik effect," accessed August 11, 2013, http://www.merriam-webster.com/medical/zeigarnik%20effect.
2. Bluma Zeigarnik (1900–1988), a Russian psychologist, first described the Zeigarnik effect in her 1927 doctoral thesis.

Chapter 4/Tool #3: Prioritize and Triage

1. *Merriam-Webster OnLine*, s.v. "priority," accessed August 11, 2013, http://www.merriam-webster.com/dictionary/priority.
2. Stephen R. Covey, *The 7 Habits of Highly Effective People: Restoring the Character Ethic* (New York, NY: Fireside, 1989).

Chapter 4/Tool #5: Reign In the Multitasking

1. Mihaly Csikszentmihalyi is one the main contributors to understanding the concept of flow and has authored many books on the subject.
2. Mihaly Csikszentmihalyi, *Finding Flow: The Psychology of Engagement with Everyday Life* (New York, NY: Basic Books, 1997).

Chapter 5/Tool #8: Tame the Inner Critics

1. The inner critic is a concept that refers to an inner voice of doubt and other limiting beliefs. This concept is commonly taught to coaches. In my case, I first learned about inner critics in Adler International Learning's coaching program.

Chapter 5/Tool #10: Ask, "What Can I Do Now?"

1. Kim George is a coach, author of several books, and founder of the Abundance Intelligence Institute®.
2. Kim George, *Coaching into Greatness: 4 Steps to Success in Business and Life* (Hoboken, NJ: Wiley & Sons, 2006).
3. The Abundance Institute®, www.abundanceintelligence.com.

Chapter 5/Tool #11: Use Powerful Questions

1. While asking powerful questions is public domain, the term *powerful questions* is a common one used by coaches and is one of the main tools taught in coaching schools.
2. Marilee Adams is the founder of the Inquiry Institute.
3. The Inquiry Institute, www. inquiryinstitute.com.
4. Marilee Adams, *Change Your Questions, Change Your Life* (San Francisco, CA: Berrett-Koehler Publishers Inc., 2009).
5. The judger and learner mindsets are distinctions that Marilee Adams makes in her work.

Chapter 5/Tool #13: Clear the Cache

1. Dr. Herbert Benson, MD, is a pioneer in mind-body medicine; founder of the Mind/Body Medical Institute at Massachusetts General Hospital in Boston; and author of many books in this field. He is also director emeritus of the Benson-Henry Institute (BHI) and a professor of medicine at Harvard Medical School.

2. Dr. Herbert Benson and William Proctor, *The Breakout Principle* (New York, NY: Scribner/Simon & Schuster, 2003).

3. *Globe and Mail*, Canada's national newspaper, www.globeandmail. com.

Chapter 5/Tool #14: Check Your Positivity Ratio

1. Sonja Lyubomirsky, PhD, is a renowned expert in the field of happiness. She is a professor of psychology at the University of California–Riverside.

2. Sonja Lyubomirsky, *The How of Happiness* (New York, NY: Penguin Press, 2007).

3. Sonja Lyubomirsky, *The Myths of Happiness: What Should Make You Happy but Doesn't; What Shouldn't Make You Happy but Does* (New York, NY: Penguin Press, 2013).

4. Barbara Fredrickson is a renowned expert in positivity and Kenan distinguished professor of psychology and award-winning director of the Positive Emotions and Psychophysiology Laboratory at the University of North Carolina.

5. Barbara Fredrickson, *Positivity* (New York, NY: Crown Publishers, 2009).

6. Barbara Fredrickson, *Love 2.0* (New York, NY: Penguin Group, 2013).

7. The term *Stepford* refers to the idea of perfect people who are actually robots and not real human beings, as depicted in the movie *The Stepford Wives* (original 1975; remake 2004).

Chapter 5/Tool #15: Create a Happiness Portfolio

1. Canadian Positive Psychology Conference (July 2012), http://www.positivepsychologycanada.com/conference2012.

2. Martin Seligman is considered the founder of the positive psychology movement. In 1996, he was elected president of the American Psychological Association by the largest vote in the organization's history. Each APA president is asked to choose a central theme for his or her term, and Seligman selected positive psychology and ushered in a new era of psychology that concentrates on what makes people feel happy and fulfilled (versus what ails). Today, Seligman is the director of the Positive Psychology Center at the University of Pennsylvania.

3. Martin Seligman, *Authentic Happiness* (New York, NY: Free Press, Division of Simon & Schuster, Inc., 2002).

4. Martin Seligman, *Flourish* (New York, NY: Free Press, Division of Simon & Schuster, Inc., 2011).

5. The five pillars Seligman speaks of in *Flourish* include hedonic pursuits (pleasure); engagement; good relationships; meaning and purpose; and accomplishments.

6. See www.VIAcharacter.org to learn about character and signature strengths and to take the assessment.

7. Christopher Peterson (1950–2012) was one of the founders of positive psychology. He was the Arthur F. Thurnau professor of psychology at the University of Michigan in Ann Arbor, Michigan, and the former chair of the clinical psychology department. He was science director of the VIA Institute on Character and co-author of *Character Strengths and Virtues*, which deals with the classification of character strengths. He is noted for his work in the study of optimism, health, character, and well-being.

8. Christopher Peterson, *A Primer in Positive Psychology* (New York, NY: Oxford University Press, 2006).

9. Christopher Peterson, *Pursuing the Good Life: 100 Reflections in Positive Psychology* (New York, NY: Oxford University Press, 2013).

Chapter 5/Tool #16: Develop the Positivity Habit

1. Shawn Achor, "Positive Intelligence," *Harvard Business Review*, January 2012.

2. Tools such as "Three Good Things," "What Went Well," and gratitude lists are widely used among positive-psychology practitioners, including coaches, therapists, educators, and others.

3. Exercises such as "Three Good Things," "What Went Well," and gratitude lists have all been extensively used and researched by many within the field of positive psychology. The ta-da list is something I created, although I have since heard others have as well (is there ever an original idea?).

Chapter 5/Tool #17: Get to Sleep

1. Aileen Burford-Mason, PhD, is a scientist and orthomolecular nutritional expert. See the following website for more information: http://aileenburfordmason.ca.

2. Aileen Burford-Mason with Judy Stoffman, *Eat Well, Age Better* (Markham, Ontario: Thomas Allen Publishers, 2012).

3. "Sleep in America" poll, National Sleep Foundation, 2013, http://www.sleepfoundation.org/2013poll.

About the Author

Eileen Chadnick, PCC, ACPC, ABC, is principal of Big Cheese Coaching, which she established in 2003. A certified coach, Eileen is a champion for personal, professional, and organizational well-being. Eileen brings a multidisciplined focus to her work, drawing from diverse fields, including emotional intelligence, positive psychology, and neuroscience, to help leaders more powerfully navigate the opportunities, goals, and challenges within their work and life and create more-meaningful experiences for themselves and others.

Eileen is a recipient of an International Coach Federation Prism Award, which recognizes excellence in leadership and performance coaching. Eileen is a contributing writer with Canada's national newspaper, the *Globe and Mail*, regularly featured as an "Ask a Coach" expert. She is also a frequent contributor to a variety of media on issues related to careers, leadership, and well-being.

Eileen completed certification at the school of Adler International and earned her PCC credential from the International Coaching Federation (ICF). She holds a bachelor of education from McGill University, with a major in fitness. Earlier in her career, she taught fitness and wellness for eight years.

In addition to her work with Big Cheese Coaching, Eileen successfully operated her own public relations and communications consulting business for fifteen years. Prior, Eileen worked at leading public relations agencies (Hill and Knowlton, and Environics Communications), a

Canadian bank, and a financial services payments association. Over the years, she has served a wide roster of top-tier clients in financial services, business and consumer products, education, and other sectors.

Outside of her work, Eileen loves to cook, eat well, go to movies and the theatre, and read good books. She plays golf irregularly (with no apologies), hikes, runs (which she has done for more than thirty years), and works out at the gym. She speaks "cat" in at least two languages, loves animals, and is blessed with an abundance of people who matter to her. Her VIA signature strengths include gratitude, creativity, curiosity, love of learning, and honesty (really, it's true). See more at www. BigCheeseCoaching.com and www.EaseRX.com.

CPSIA information can be obtained
at www.ICGtesting.com
Printed in the USA
LVOW11s1925161216
517654LV00001B/9/P